How to Build Wealth, Gain Freedom,
and Live Life on Your Own Terms

# RETIRE BY 30

*Foreword by Grant Sabatier*

## CODY BERMAN

ISBN: 979-8-90057-179-9 - Ebook

ISBN: 979-8-90057-180-5 - Paperback

# GET YOUR FREE GIFT!

This book references a lot of resources—websites, calculators, tools, and more. Instead of flipping back through pages trying to find them later, I've compiled everything into one place for you. Think of this as your toolkit for early retirement.

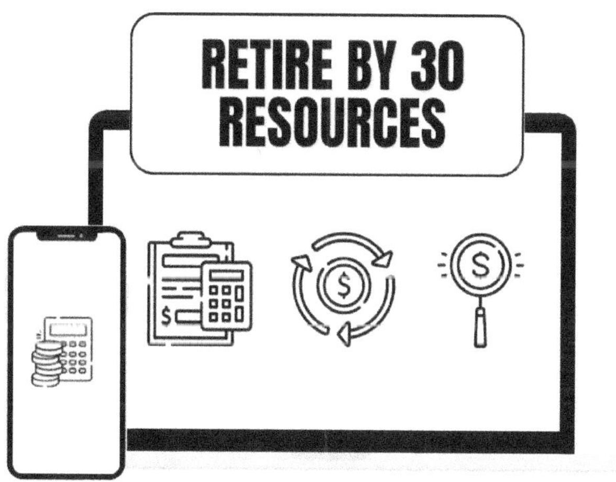


You can get a copy by visiting:
retireby30book.com/resources

# DEDICATION

To my dad, Alan — who always supported and believed in me in everything I did. Even though you thought it was "impossible" for someone to retire in their 20s, I know you'd be proud of me, and I'm grateful I could prove you wrong. I wish more than anything that you could see where I am today. Rest in peace.

To my mom, Ruth — my biggest fan. Thank you for always supporting me through my toughest decisions and for shaping me into the person I am today.

To my wife, Lauren — thank you for believing in me through every phase of this journey. From the moment I had the crazy idea to retire early, through quitting my job, and everything since, you've never wavered. I love you, and I couldn't imagine sharing this adventure with anyone else.

To my brother, Sam — for always having my back and being a soundboard for all my wild ideas.

And to all my family and friends who've supported me from the start — there are too many to name, but you know who you are. I'm so grateful for each and every one of you.

I consider myself incredibly lucky to have such an amazing support network. Thank you for believing in me and helping make this journey possible.

# CONTENTS

## Section 5: Early Retirement

# FOREWORD

Written by Grant Sabatier, author of *Financial Freedom* and *Inner Entrepreneur*

We slowed at a stop sign outside Mobile, Alabama, when I saw a guy jump into his car and heard someone yell, "Hey, where are you going?" We'd taken a wrong turn and landed somewhere we clearly weren't welcome.

A car started chasing us, trying to force us to pull over. I blew through stop sign after stop sign in our 1981 VW camper van, heart pounding, convinced we were about to get robbed—or worse. I finally spotted a freeway entrance and floored it, losing them as we merged into traffic.

There have only been a few moments in my life when I've had that cold, final "this is it" feeling. That was one of them.

Cody was in the passenger seat, laughing.

Not nervous laughter. Not denial. Just pure, unfazed calm in the face of uncertainty.

That's Cody.

He has a joy for living I've rarely seen. There was no version of his life where he was going to sit in a cubicle for 40 years just because that's what you're "supposed" to do. Some people want more from life—more freedom, more ownership, more control. If you're holding this book, you're probably one of them. Cody definitely is.

After knowing him for about a month, I saw the drive. He was curious, hungry to learn, and willing to do the work. So I asked if he wanted to help coordinate my book tour across the U.S. and Canada for *Financial Freedom*. He said yes—and then quit his job to join me.

We spent three months on the road and did more than 80 events. I had already reached financial independence. Cody was just getting started. During ten-hour drives between cities, he'd pepper me with questions. How did you negotiate this? Why invest that way? What would you do differently? I told him everything. No gatekeeping. No secrets.

What I didn't expect was how fast he'd move and reach financial independence.

When I first met Cody, he wasn't chasing status. He was chasing freedom. Most people say they want to be rich, but what they actually want is control over their time. They want to wake up without an alarm. Take a Tuesday off without asking permission. Spend more time with their family. Choose the work they do and who they do it with.

That's financial independence. Not a flashy lifestyle. Not a number in an account. It's the ability to choose your life instead of having it chosen for you.

This book lays out a practical system to get there. There's no fluff here. Just clear tactics, real stories, and the decisions that actually move the needle.

The math is simple: increase the gap between what you earn and what you spend. Invest the difference. Repeat. Let compounding work. Avoid catastrophic mistakes. Stay consistent long enough for the math to do its job. Simple doesn't mean easy—but it does mean possible.

Cody didn't stumble into financial freedom. He engineered it.

He understood something most people miss: retirement is not an age—it's a number. More importantly, it's a strategy. He optimized the big levers—housing, transportation, income. He widened the gap. He resisted lifestyle inflation as his earnings grew. He built systems instead of relying on motivation. That's what works. That's what this book teaches.

But here's the part that matters most: financial independence is not the finish line. It's the starting line.

We only get one life. You can spend decades trading time for money and hope you're healthy enough to enjoy what's left. Or you can make intentional trade-offs now that buy you decades of optionality later.

It took me five years, from 25 to 30, to reach financial independence. I made sacrifices. But if that bought me 50-plus years of freedom, that's a 900% return on investment. I'll take that every time. Being able to spend unlimited time with my daughter at 40 without worrying about money is the greatest gift I could have given myself. The experiences I've been able to have and how my life has expanded simply because I have options is remarkable.

Many people today are underprepared and burned out. Hope is not a strategy. This book gives you one. It will challenge you to confront your spending honestly, increase your income instead of obsessing over minor expenses, treat debt as math—not shame—and focus on the few big decisions that actually change your trajectory. You only need to do a few of the tactics in this book to get 80% of the results - the sum is greater than the parts.

The path isn't glamorous. You might drive an older car. Share housing. Choose long-term freedom over short-term validation. But those decisions compound quickly. Eventually, work becomes optional. And when that day comes, you'll realize the real reward wasn't the money—it was time. You can make more money. You cannot make more time.

You don't have to retire at 30. That's not the point. The point is optionality. The point is freedom. Cody is living proof. I've watched him build it—and now he's showing you how.

As you turn the page, don't just ask how to reach financial independence. Ask the better question: how are you going to use your freedom?

# THE AMERICAN NIGHTMARE

*"It's called the American Dream because you have to be asleep to believe it."*

— George Carlin

At 5 a.m., my alarm would go off, and I'd already feel behind. I'd stumble into the shower and get ready for my day. Then I'd make breakfast and catch the 6:30 a.m. train from the suburbs into Boston. That hour and a half on the train was the only "free" time I'd have until my train home later that day, and I spent it working on side hustles and business ideas. I was doing everything in my power to increase my income.

By 8:15 a.m., I'd step off the train and make the fifteen-minute walk through the city to my office, where I worked for a commercial real estate company. From 8:30 a.m. to 5:30 p.m., I sat behind a computer, punching numbers into Excel, counting the minutes until I could leave. Then I'd hop back on the train to work on my side hustles for another couple of hours. From the train station, I'd go straight to the gym, get home around 9 p.m., eat dinner, maybe squeeze in a little more side hustle work, and collapse into bed around 10 p.m.—just to do it all over again the next day.

I was twenty-two years old, working twelve- to fourteen-hour days, and already exhausted by the idea that this was what life was supposed to look like.

Everyone around me said I was "crushing it." I'd graduated from college, landed an $80,000-a-year job right out of school, and had a clear career path ahead of me. From the outside, I was living the dream. But every morning on that train, I felt like I was sprinting toward a finish line I didn't even want to cross.

My coworkers were burned out, my bosses were always stressed, and even the executives, the ones I was supposedly working so hard to become, didn't seem happy. I looked at my boss, my boss's boss, and even my boss's boss's boss, and realized I didn't want any of their lives.

I didn't understand. I had done everything "right"—a college degree, a good salary, and solid savings. But I still felt stuck. I wasn't living the American Dream. I was living the American Nightmare.

My story didn't start here, though. Long before that train ride into Boston, hope-filled dreams were already taking root and were slowly but surely breaking through. I began questioning the American Dream and plotting out a dream of my own.

## The Spark

In early 2016, my mom recommended that I read *The 4-Hour Workweek* by Tim Ferriss, and it completely rewired how I thought about work and money. Up to that point, I believed "success" meant climbing the corporate ladder, getting promotions, and maybe one day earning $100+ an hour as a doctor, lawyer, or financier. But Tim talked about achieving freedom, creating automation, and building income streams that worked *without you*. That single idea, that the richest people don't trade time for money, hit me hard.

I didn't realize it then, but that book planted the first seed of what would eventually grow into financial independence.

A year later, in 2017, I stumbled across the *Mr. Money Mustache* blog, and the article that changed everything was called *The Shockingly Simple Math Behind Early Retirement*. It was the first time I'd seen financial freedom broken down into something measurable and concrete (more on that in the next chapter). The math showed that if you could save half your income, you could retire in 17 years. Save 70%, and it could be closer to 8 or 9. That's when it clicked for me. Retirement wasn't an age. It was *a number.*

That realization turned into obsession. I devoured every book, blog post, podcast, YouTube video, and Reddit thread I could find. I started running my own numbers, imagining what it would take to quit my job before 30.

At the time, I was still in school, getting ready to graduate. But I already knew one thing: I didn't want the traditional path. I didn't want to grind for 40 years and wait until my mid-60s to finally "enjoy" life. I wanted more time *now*, not decades from now.

I didn't know exactly *how* at the time, but I knew there was a different way. And a few years later, when I found myself deep in that Boston grind, those early lessons would come rushing back and change everything.

## The Plan

After discovering financial independence, I knew I needed a plan. The math was simple enough: save a ton of money, invest it wisely, and eventually, I'd never have to work again. An escape plan wasn't enough. I wanted a strategy.

When I graduated from college, I made a deliberate choice to take a high-paying corporate job in commercial real estate lending. It wasn't my dream career, but it was strategic. The salary was $80,000 a year—more money than I'd ever made— and I saw it as my launchpad to financial independence. At the same time, I was already making about $1,200 per month from my side hustles. That combination gave me a real shot at saving aggressively.

In my head, the plan was straightforward:

- Work in corporate America for 7 to 10 years.

- Save and invest every dollar I could.

- Hit financial independence by 30.

The spreadsheets made it clear: if I stayed disciplined, I could retire by 30. I just had to live on a fraction of my income, invest the rest, and keep building side hustles. I became determined—borderline obsessed—with making it happen. It felt realistic, logical, and responsible.

But here's the thing — that's *not* how it went.

## The Leap

Okay, now back to where we started — in Boston.

Remember that 6:30 a.m. train, the long hours, and the endless grind? Now you know why I took that job in the first place. It wasn't because I loved commercial real estate. It was because I thought it was my ticket to financial independence. I was willing to grind for several years if it meant freedom later, but things didn't quite play out that way.

I had a great salary, a promising career, and a clear path upward. But inside, I felt drained. The stress, the commute, the seemingly pointless work — it was slowly crushing my motivation. Every morning on that 6:30 a.m. train, I'd ask myself: *"Is this really worth it?"*

At first, I told myself it was temporary, that I could push through for a few years, save like crazy, and use this job to retire by 30. But deep down, I already knew I wasn't built for this. I didn't want to spend my twenties waiting for my thirties to begin. So I made the hardest and best decision of my life: I quit.

I remember walking into my boss's office to tell him about my plan to pursue entrepreneurship, and being told I was a "waste of time and resources." So much for the support. Those words fueled me more than he'll ever know.

Looking back, it wasn't a reckless move. I had built up a $35,000 financial cushion, which covered years of living expenses at the time. (Yes, I was insanely frugal—some might say too frugal.) That money gave me the confidence to take a mini-retirement and figure out what was next.

Still, it was terrifying. I remember walking out of the office on my last day with a strange mix of fear and freedom. My coworkers were confused, my bosses were angry, but for the first time in my adult life, I felt completely free.

The next few months became a blur of exploration and growth. I traveled, met new people, and reconnected with my curiosity. That time off gave me space to think deeply about what I actually wanted my life to look like, and it led to everything that came next. I took a three-month book tour across the

U.S. with my friend and mentor Grant Sabatier, launched my digital products business, Gold City Ventures, with my friend Julie Berninger, and eventually built a life entirely on my own terms.

Quitting my job wasn't the end of my financial independence journey. It was the moment it truly began.

## The Climb

When I quit my corporate job, I didn't know exactly what was next, but I knew I wasn't going back. I had my mini-retirement cushion, my side hustles, and a ridiculous work ethic. Over the next three years, I went all-in on entrepreneurship, real estate, and investing. My digital products business took off. I bought rental properties. I doubled down on learning, experimenting, and stacking wins. It was the same energy I once poured into my 9-to-5, but now I was building my own freedom instead of someone else's.

My income doubled every single year.

2019: $96,000
2020: $198,000
2021: $403,000

But instead of inflating my lifestyle, I did the opposite. I kept my monthly expenses around $2,000 and saved more than 80% of my income. My annual expenses were just $24,000 in the same year I made over $400,000.

Yes, it was extreme. But those short-term sacrifices bought me something priceless—permanent freedom.

Three years after walking away from corporate America, I officially hit financial independence at age 25. I had $500,000 invested in the stock market, $3,700 a month coming in from rental properties, and a digital products business bringing in over $10,000 a month in passive income. Work became optional. And for the first time, I wasn't chasing an escape. I was designing a life I actually wanted to live.

## Now, It's Your Turn

If you're reading this, chances are that you, too, have wondered, *"Is this really what the rest of my life looks like?"*

You work hard, save what you can, and do everything you're "supposed" to, but you're still stuck on the treadmill. You're told to save for retirement, but that retirement is decades away—or so you've thought. Whether you're 18 and just starting, a single parent juggling three kids, stuck in a low-paying job, buried in debt, or anywhere in between, early retirement *is* possible.

As you've seen, I didn't win the lottery or hit it big overnight. I learned how to play the game differently—how to earn more, spend intentionally, invest early, and build systems that make money work for me instead of the other way around. This book will show you how to do the same.

You don't have to be an entrepreneur, buy real estate, sell digital products, or do any of the exact things I did. That's not the point of this book. The point is to give you the tools, mindset, and strategies to reach financial independence and retire early on your own terms. Whether that means investing in index funds, starting a side hustle, or simply learning to live below your means, there's no one "right" way to get there. The path will look different for everyone, but the destination is the same: freedom.

We'll start with some basic principles in Section 1, such as FIRE, and the gap between income and expenses. From there, we'll cover how to widen that gap in Sections 2–4. Section 2 addresses your expenses and how to keep them minimal. Section 3 looks at increasing your income. Section 4 covers investing in simple, proven ways that grow your wealth over time. You'll discover how to use index funds, real estate, and smart tax strategies to accelerate your path.

*Retire by 30* is different from most personal finance books. This isn't a collection of abstract theories or overly complex strategies. You'll learn the exact approaches I used to make work optional by 25 and build a multi million dollar net worth by 30. No gatekeeping. No fluff. Just practical strategies that actually worked in the real world.

But this book isn't just about money—it's about choice. It isn't only about quitting work; it's about creating options through financial independence. Whether you want to travel the world, pursue your passion, or completely reinvent your life, this book will help you build that freedom. By the time you're done reading, you'll not only understand the math behind financial independence, you'll understand how to use it to build a life you actually want to live.

# THE BASICS

# CHAPTER 1

# FIRE

*"You can have anything you want, but not everything you want."*

— VICKI ROBIN

Until I discovered financial independence, I always thought the richest people were the ones driving Lamborghinis, living in mansions, and flying on private jets. In reality, the richest people are the ones who can go to the beach on a random Tuesday, take a month-long vacation at the drop of a hat, and never worry about paying the bills. Money isn't the goal—freedom is. Freedom to do what you want, with who you want, when you want. Financial independence is about having options, not just a pile of money.

## A Quick History of FIRE

First thing's first—definitions.

FIRE stands for Financial Independence, Retire Early.

We'll be using this acronym throughout the book to save some ink.

The idea of financial independence isn't new. Plato and Socrates discussed it in 400 BCE. Henry David Thoreau wrote about it in the mid-1850s. But the modern version of FIRE took off thanks to books like *Your Money or Your Life* by Vicki Robin and *The Simple Path to Wealth* by JL Collins, blogs like Mr. Money Mustache and The Mad Fientist, and podcasts like ChooseFI and Afford Anything. It challenged the traditional idea that you must work until 65, and instead introduced the idea of aligning spending with values, tracking your life energy (time), and reaching financial independence well before "normal" retirement age.

Today, millions of *normal* people have reached financial independence and retired early. They look ordinary on the surface—normal homes, normal cars, normal lives—but they made a few simple decisions that set them on a completely different path. Once I realized that, I couldn't stop asking how they pulled it off.

The "millionaire next door" was a real thing. But how? How could anyone possibly retire in their 20s, 30s, or 40s? Why didn't my family know about this? Why didn't my friends know about this? Why didn't they teach us about this in school? I was determined to find out.

One chart in particular blew my mind. It was from an article published in 2012 by Mr. Money Mustache called, "The Shockingly Simple Math Behind Early Retirement".

| Savings Rate (Percent) | Working Years Until Retirement |
|---|---|
| 5 | 66 |
| 10 | 51 |
| 15 | 43 |
| 20 | 37 |
| 25 | 32 |
| 30 | 28 |
| 35 | 25 |
| 40 | 22 |
| 45 | 19 |
| 50 | 17 |
| 55 | 14.5 |
| 60 | 12.5 |
| 65 | 10.5 |
| 70 | 8.5 |
| 75 | 7 |
| 80 | 5.5 |
| 85 | 4 |
| 90 | Under 3 |
| 95 | Under 2 |
| 100 | Zero |

As defined by the article, your savings rate is calculated by how much money you spend as a percentage of how much money you earn each year.

So if you're earning $100,000, spending $80,000, and saving $20,000, your savings rate is 20%. At that savings rate, you'll be able to retire in 37 years or less.

Depending on your personality, this chart could either excite you or scare the life out of you. When I first saw this chart, I thought, "Wow, if I could save 80% of my income, I could retire in 5.5 years!" For others, you might see this chart and realize you aren't saving nearly enough.

No matter how this chart makes you feel, there are other ways of achieving financial independence that don't involve saving such a high percentage of your income. We'll discuss the different methods in this chapter and throughout the entire book.

## Two Main Paths to FIRE

There are two main ways to reach FIRE:

*1. Nest Egg Method*

This is the more "traditional" path in the FI world. Basically, you save up a big investment portfolio and then live off a small percentage of it every year.

Here's the basic math:

- Take your annual expenses and multiply that number by 25

- Or take your monthly expenses and multiply them by 300

The answer to either of those equations determines your "FI number".

For example, if you spend $60,000 per year, your FI number would be $1,500,000, meaning that you'd need a million and a half dollars invested to fund your current lifestyle.

| Monthly Spending | Annual Spending | FI Number |
| --- | --- | --- |
| $2,000 | $24,000 | $600,000 |
| $3,000 | $36,000 | $900,000 |
| $4,000 | $48,000 | $1,200,000 |
| $5,000 | $60,000 | $1,500,000 |
| $6,000 | $72,000 | $1,800,000 |
| $7,000 | $84,000 | $2,100,000 |
| $8,000 | $96,000 | $2,400,000 |
| $9,000 | $108,000 | $2,700,000 |
| $10,000 | $120,000 | $3,000,000 |

These numbers are based on the 4% rule, which found that if you withdraw 4% of your portfolio each year in retirement, adjusting that amount each year for inflation, your money is very likely to last for the rest of your life. In fact, many simulations show retirees finishing with 2–10 times their starting balance, even while withdrawing the entire time.

If you really want to nerd out about the origins of the 4% rule, you can read the Trinity Study, which was an influential paper in retirement planning, informally named after the Trinity University professors who authored it in 1998. It's also known as "Retirement Spending: Choosing a Sustainable Withdrawal Rate". The study explored how much retirees could safely withdraw from their investment portfolios each year without running out of money during their retirement.

The Trinity Study looked at historical market data going all the way back to 1926. It tested different withdrawal rates across dozens of market scenarios—bull markets, crashes, inflationary periods—and found that a 4% withdrawal rate worked in nearly all of them.

In other words, it's not about timing the market perfectly. It's about relying on long-term historical averages. And that's why the 4% rule has become a foundational principle in the FI community. When you base your FI number on this rule, you're not hoping everything goes right; you're planning based on 100+ years of data.

### 2. Cash Flow Method

The other approach to reaching FI is what I like to call the Cash Flow Method. Instead of building up a massive investment portfolio and using the 4% rule like the Nest Egg Method, the goal here is to replace your monthly expenses with passive—or at least mostly passive—cash flow.

Most of the ways to create passive cash flow involve either buying, building, or managing some type of asset or business.

Here are a few examples:

- Rental properties (long-term rentals, short-term rentals)
- Digital products (printables, ebooks, templates)

- Small businesses (laundromats, car washes, vending machines)

- Online businesses (courses, memberships, service-based)

- Stock market dividends

While this approach is a bit more hands-on than the Nest Egg Method, it's also a lot faster.

I've seen some people reach financial independence in as little as two years from their real estate cash flow. Other people are making $5,000+ in mostly passive income each month selling digital products. There are a lot of ways to build passive cash flow, and we'll discuss them at length in the *Income* section of this book.

When it comes to choosing between the Nest Egg and Cash Flow Methods, you don't actually have to choose one or the other. When I hit FI in 2021, it was through a hybrid approach. I had built up over $500,000 in stock market investments (Nest Egg Method), but I also had $10,000+ per month in passive income coming in from my digital products and online businesses, plus another $3,000+ per month from my rental properties (Cash Flow Method).

For *most* people aiming to retire in under ten years, some form of cash flow is essential—because building a massive nest egg quickly usually requires an extraordinary income. This book contains a menu of options to choose from to best fit your lifestyle, strengths, and current situation.

## Retirement is a Number, Not an Age

Most people, myself included, were brainwashed into thinking that retirement was an age. Even the phrase "retirement age" is a pretty standard synonym for "65+". But the truth is, retirement is a number, not an age.

The numbers in your investment accounts and the passive income from your businesses don't care how old you are. Math is math. Whether you choose the Nest Egg Method, Cash Flow Method, or some combination of the two, the numbers don't change based on age.

There are actually some advantages to retiring early that we'll discuss later in this book, despite the government's best efforts to keep you working until your later years with their subsidized health insurance, early withdrawal penalties, and elderly assistance programs.

Now you might be thinking, "If I retire early, what am I supposed to do with the rest of my life?!" Retiring doesn't mean you can never work again. You can still work, or not. It's completely up to you. The key difference about working after reaching FI is that you *choose* to work because it excites or fulfills you. You're not *obligated* to work to pay the bills.

Some people are perfectly content just hanging out, relaxing, and enjoying the fruits of their early retirement. But in my experience, anyone who has the drive and willpower to retire in their 20s, 30s, or 40s is typically not someone who likes to sit around.

Since I've reached financial independence, I still work, but on my own terms. I'm able to have complete control over my time and focus on the things that really matter to me.

## Traditional Retirement is Broken

Traditional retirement is not what it used to be. Gone are the days of the cushy company pension and generous social security checks.

Unfortunately, most people go through life saving almost nothing and fully expecting to be taken care of by their company or government.

Here are a few facts that might alarm you:

- 45% of Americans have *nothing* saved for retirement.

- In 2025, the average Social Security benefit was just $2,008 per month or ~$24,000 per year.

- Only 15% of private-sector workers have a traditional pension

- The median 401(k) balance at retirement is $95,425

People are entering retirement less prepared than ever, and to make matters worse, they're living longer while costs keep rising. Unless you're one of the lucky few with a cushy government pension, your retirement is entirely in your hands.

Luckily, this book is also in your hands, so you'll be well equipped to reach financial independence and retire comfortably.

## Customizing Your FI Plan

Not all financial advice fits everyone, and that's okay. Some people love the simplicity of index fund investing. Others thrive on building and scaling cash-flowing businesses. What matters most is that your approach to FI aligns with your personality, your goals, and your lifestyle.

Personal finance is just that: personal. Choose a path that works for *you*. Your risk tolerance, your income sources, and your timeline should all influence your FI plan. Furthermore, it's okay for your plan to change. In my first job out of college as a commercial real estate lender, I built a detailed spreadsheet outlining a seven-year path to retirement, aiming to be done by age 29. I had every year's income and expenses mapped out.

But life took a turn, and I left that job after just seven months and eventually decided to pursue entrepreneurship full-time. My FI plan shifted dramatically, but the transition wasn't too hard because I had already started moving in the right direction with a solid plan in place. It's a lot easier to turn a ship in motion than one that's still sitting in the sand.

## This Isn't Just About Money

At the end of the day, FI isn't about numbers; it's about freedom. It's about waking up and spending your time how you want, not how your employer tells you to.

For me, that means spreading financial literacy, working on passion projects, spending time with friends and family, and traveling the world. I get to build my days around what lights me up, not what shows up on a meeting calendar. For you, it might mean something totally different, and that's the beauty of it.

Money might not buy happiness, but it *can* buy freedom. Imagine not stressing over bills, missing out on fun with friends, or figuring out how to beg for time off just to take a group trip. FI gives you options, and options are what create a truly rich life.

This is the power of financial independence. It's not about hoarding money. It's not about yachts, luxury cars, and designer clothes. It's about aligning your time, energy, and money with what matters most to you.

## Call to Action: Find Your "Why"

Take a moment and get clear on why you want financial freedom.

Are you trying to escape a toxic job? Spend more time with your kids? Travel the world? Dive into a passion project? Stop stressing about money?

Your answer becomes your north star. When things get hard or uncomfortable, this is the "why" that will make all the tactics in this book worth it.

# CHAPTER 2

# THE GAP

*"Building wealth has little to do with your income or investment returns, and lots to do with your savings rate."*

— MORGAN HOUSEL

The gap between your income and your expenses is the engine that powers your journey to financial independence. It's not how much you earn. It's not how much you cut back. It's the difference between the two—the space in between—that determines how fast you can reach your goals.

The gap is your fuel. It's the money left over after you've covered your basic needs, wants, and responsibilities. It's the money you'll invest to reach financial independence.

## Income - Expenses = The Gap

Sounds simple enough, right? This little equation is more powerful than it seems. It determines how much you can invest, how fast you can grow wealth, and ultimately, how soon you can walk away from work that no longer serves you.

Think of the gap as your personal launchpad. A bigger gap means faster progress toward FI. A smaller gap means a longer road and more risk of burnout.

Here's an example:

- Income: $5,000/month

- Expenses: $4,000/month

- The Gap: $1,000/month

- Savings Rate: 20%

The bigger the gap between your income and your expenses, the sooner you can retire.

**Maximizing the gap was the single biggest lever I pulled on my way to financial independence.** You can make all the income in the world, but if you spend it all, you're stuck. The gap is what gives you freedom.

Don't worry, you don't have to live frugally and maximize the gap forever. Once you reach FI, you can loosen the reins and spend more freely on what you truly value. The key is keeping that gap as wide as possible in the early years, when it has the biggest impact on how fast you reach financial freedom.

## Why the Gap Matters

Let's bust one of the biggest myths in personal finance: income alone builds wealth. You can make $400,000 a year and still be broke if you're spending $395,000. I've met people like this. On the flip side, someone earning $50,000 and saving $20,000 is crushing it. That person has options. That person is building freedom. It's not about income alone—it's about how much of that income you keep.

During the last six months of my corporate job, I made $44,000 and spent only $9,000 of it. My gap was $35,000, and my savings rate was almost 80% during that period. I was living cheaply, side hustling like crazy, and saving as much as I could. These numbers sound unbelievable, but I cover them in depth in the Expense section of the book coming up.

For the next three years, as my income jumped to $96,000, then $192,000, then $403,000, my expenses stayed almost exactly the same: $2,000 per month. At the end of those three years, I reached financial independence.

It wasn't because I struck gold, discovered some secret investment strategy, or had a windfall. It was because I relentlessly protected the gap.

## How to Widen the Gap

There are only two levers you can pull to widen the gap: increase your income, or decrease your expenses.

Most people focus on just one, but if you're serious about financial independence, you need to explore both.

*Increase Income*

You can widen the gap by:

- Picking up a side hustle (gig work, freelancing, selling digital products, etc.)

- Negotiating a raise or promotion

- Switching jobs or industries

- Building a business

- Investing in income-producing assets (real estate, dividends, etc.)

During my journey to FI, I tried 30+ side hustles. I was doing absolutely everything to boost my income: selling digital products, cleaning boats, blogging, podcast editing, freelance writing, landscaping, disc golf manufacturing…you name it. At one point, I was doing Uber Eats deliveries on a beat-up bike in Australia. I got a couple one-star reviews for sweating on people's food.

Pro Tip: Don't do Uber Eats on a one-gear bike in a hilly area.

Eventually, I landed on digital products and real estate as my main income sources. But in the early days, I was just trying to earn an extra $100-$200 here and there, because every dollar mattered.

Even $200 in additional income per month equates to $2,400 per year, and—using our $20,000 lifestyle example from earlier—this means a 12% savings rate increase. That kind of boost can shave years off your retirement timeline.

*Decrease Expenses*

You can also widen the gap by cutting expenses:

- House hacking (renting out the spare rooms/units in your house)

- Driving a paid-off car instead of leasing or financing

- Cooking at home instead of eating out

- Cutting unused subscriptions

- Being intentional about every dollar

To decrease my expenses, I lived in a one-bedroom apartment while house hacking, drove a paid-off car, and reduced my food and subscription costs to the essentials.

I didn't feel deprived. My girlfriend (now wife) and I still traveled, had fun, and lived a full life. But we were intentional. We kept housing cheap, avoided lifestyle creep, and made the frugal choices that aligned with our values. Frugality doesn't mean deprivation. It means prioritization.

## The Power of the Gap

Your gap is what allows you to invest. In year three of my FI journey, my income hit $403,000, but I didn't inflate my lifestyle. I could have moved to a luxury apartment. I could have upgraded my car. I could have bought a Rolex. But I didn't. Instead, I continued to live on ~$2,000 per month and invest aggressively.

To demonstrate the power of the gap, let's look at Joe and Jane. (Pretend that taxes don't exist for a second, for simplicity's sake.) Joe makes $100,000 per year, spends $95,000, and invests the $5,000 gap each year. Jane also makes $100,000 per year, but spends $60,000, leaving her with a $40,000 gap to invest.

|  | Joe | Jane |
| --- | --- | --- |
| Income | $100,000 | $100,000 |
| Expenses | $95,000 | $60,000 |
| Gap | $5,000 | $40,000 |
| Investment Return (%) | 8% | 8% |
| Years Invested | 30 | 30 |
| Total | $565,509 | $4,530,875 |

The difference is staggering.

Now you might be sympathizing hard with Joe right now and wondering how in the world Jane is saving 40% of her income.

Well, Joe rents an apartment downtown. Jane bought a duplex and rents out the other unit. Joe leases a new car every 3 years. Jane has been driving the same paid-off car for 7 years. Joe has an Amazon package coming almost every day with something he bought on impulse. Jane is a lot more intentional and only buys what she needs.

On the surface, their lives aren't *that* different, but after decades, Jane has almost a whopping $4 million more than Joe.

## What to Do With the Gap

Once you've created a healthy gap, you need a plan for that extra money. We cover that later in this book. In Section 4, we'll talk all about investing and how to put that money to work in index funds, real estate, and even alternative investments.

You can use your gap to:

- Build an emergency fund
- Invest in index funds
- Buy rental properties
- Launch a business
- Save for a future purchase

Each dollar has a purpose. Put it to work. The last thing you want to do with your gap is let it sit idle without a plan. Even basic investing can compound into massive growth over time.

You don't need to be a financial genius. You don't need a trust fund. You don't need to make six figures. You just need to be intentional with the space between what you earn and what you spend. That's where the magic happens. That's where freedom begins. If you protect that gap and invest it wisely, it will change your life.

## Call to Action: What's Your Gap?

Take five minutes right now to calculate your own gap:

- What's your monthly income (after tax)?

- What are your average monthly expenses?

- What's the difference?

That's your gap. If it's smaller than you'd like, don't panic. Start small. Increase your income by $100. Decrease your spending by $100. Do it again next month.

Protect your gap, grow your gap, and use it to build the life you actually want.

# SECTION 2

# EXPENSES

# CHAPTER 3

# TRACKING YOUR EXPENSES

*"What gets measured gets managed."*

— PETER DRUCKER

I haven't always tracked my spending. Early on, I assumed that if I wasn't going into credit card debt and my checking account wasn't running dry, I must be doing okay. But *okay* doesn't get you to financial independence, *intentionality* does.

According to a 2025 study conducted by Yahoo Finance, 71% of respondents didn't know how much they'd spent the previous month. It's hard to improve your spending when you don't even have a starting point. That's why tracking is so important. Once you establish a baseline for your monthly expenses, you can come up with a plan to optimize them. We'll discuss lots of cost-saving strategies in the coming chapters.

At the end of the day, your spending mirrors your priorities, whether you realize it or not. If someone looked at your last 30 days of expenses, what would they think you care about? Tracking your expenses might expose a gap between what you *think* you value and what you're *actually* spending money on. Numbers don't lie.

Once you start measuring, you can start managing. That's when things shift from "I hope I can save this month" to "I know exactly what levers I can pull to hit a 50%+ savings rate."

## Fixed vs. Variable Expenses

Let's start with a simple breakdown: some expenses don't change much from month to month (fixed), while others are more in your control (variable).

Fixed expenses include things like rent or mortgage payments, insurance premiums, student loan payments, and subscriptions. These are the "non-negotiables" in your budget, or at least they appear that way. But as you'll soon find out, many of these can still be optimized. You can refinance loans, negotiate lower insurance premiums, or cancel unused subscriptions.

Variable expenses include things like groceries, dining out, entertainment, travel, gas, and shopping. These are typically much easier to dial up and down.

If you're not sure where an expense fits, ask yourself: "Does this amount change month to month?" If it does, it's variable. If not, it's fixed. Here are a few examples:

| Fixed Expenses | Variable Expenses |
| --- | --- |
| Rent or Mortgage | Groceries |
| Property Taxes | Dining Out |
| Insurance (health, auto, home) | Gas / Fuel (if it varies month to month) |
| Internet | Travel / Vacations |
| Phone Plan | Entertainment (movies, events, concerts) |
| Car Payment | Clothing & Accessories |
| Student Loan Payments | Household Supplies |
| Gym Membership | Medical Bills (if unpredictable) |
| Childcare (fixed-rate daycare) | Gifts / Holidays / Occasions |
| Subscriptions (Netflix, Spotify, etc.) | Personal Care (haircuts, skincare, etc.) |

If the goal is to retire early, you'll want to get your fixed expenses as low as possible. This might mean changing your housing situation, downgrading your car, and taking an honest look at where you might be overspending. This process is not easy, but it *will* be worth it.

Take my friends James and Emily Lowery, for example. By all traditional money standards, they were doing great. James was working as a manager in a physical therapy clinic, and Emily was a mechanical engineer. Their combined income was

$95,000 per year. They lived in a fancy high-rise apartment, owned three separate cars, and were living the dream—from the outside at least. In reality, they were spending everything they were earning. James admitted, "We were happy if we had $1,000 in our account every month after our bills were paid."

They couldn't figure out what they were doing wrong. They were making "good money", working "good jobs", and doing everything that society told them to do to be successful. They didn't start seeing real progress until they broke their spending into separate categories and created a game plan for each one.

## Breaking Down Your Spending

Once you understand the difference between fixed and variable expenses, the next step is to categorize where your money is going. I recommend breaking it down into major buckets:

- Housing

- Transportation

- Food (groceries + dining out)

- Utilities & Services

- Healthcare & Insurance

- Entertainment & Travel

- Personal Spending (clothing, gifts, hobbies)

To get a visual of your monthly spending, create a simple pie chart or sketch one by hand. Use whatever categories make the most sense for you; there's no need to match mine exactly. You can also use apps like Empower or Monarch Money to help.

Here's a basic example:

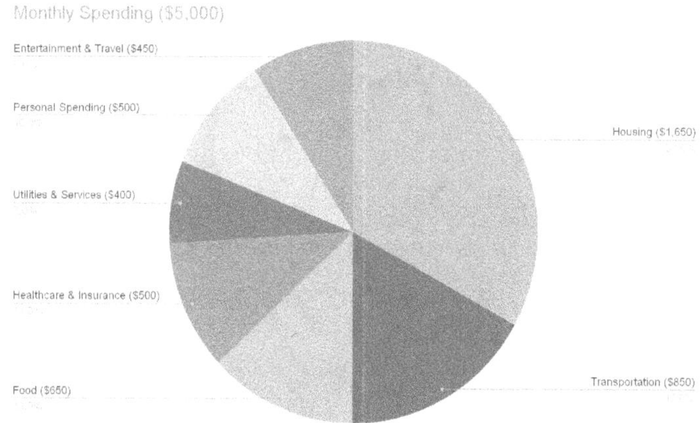


Seeing your monthly spending in this way makes it easy to see which changes will make the biggest impact. Most people overestimate how much they spend on the little stuff and underestimate the big stuff.

You've probably heard people say you need to cut out the daily coffee to build wealth. But here's the truth: your $5 latte probably isn't the problem. It's the $2,500/month rent, $700/month car payment, and $200 dinners that are killing your budget. If you optimize those, the small stuff won't matter nearly as much. Don't get lost in the $5 decisions if you haven't looked at the $1,000 ones yet.

And don't forget to account for irregular or one-time expenses like annual insurance premiums, holiday gifts, or that one big vacation. These often get ignored in monthly tracking, but can sneak up and derail your budget. A good rule of thumb is to divide those annual costs by 12 and add them to your monthly budget.

## Spend on What You Value

Now I know what some of you might be thinking: "This guy is crazy. I love where I live. I'm not changing my housing situation." or "If this whole FI thing means I need to stop buying healthy food and quit my gym membership, I'm out."

Don't worry. You don't have to optimize *everything*. You can continue to spend on what you value, and cut back on the rest. But for most people, the majority of their income goes toward things they couldn't care less about.

Here's a quick exercise: Write down the 10 things that you value most or that create the most meaning in your life. I have a screenshot on my phone from when I did this with my wife (then girlfriend), Lauren, back in April of 2020. On my "top 10 things I value" list were:

1. Time with Lauren

2. Hanging with friends & family

3. Travel

4. Fitness

5. Feeling challenged/fulfilled

6. Making an impact on people's lives

7.  Building businesses

8.  Volunteering

9.  Having high-quality things

10. Making money

Really, take a few minutes to jot down your own list. It doesn't have to be perfect.

1. _______________________________________________

2. _______________________________________________

3. _______________________________________________

4. _______________________________________________

5. _______________________________________________

6. _______________________________________________

7. _______________________________________________

8. _______________________________________________

9. _______________________________________________

10. ______________________________________________

Now compare that list to your last 30 days of spending. Use bank statements, credit card statements, or just go off memory if you don't have either of those. Are the two in sync?

I've seen some people spending $1,000/month on their car, even though "driving a nice car" didn't make their top 10 list. Others spend $700 per month on restaurants when "cooking" or "trying new recipes" made the list.

I'm not here to judge. You can spend your money however you want. Just make sure your spending is in alignment with your values. Financial independence isn't just about cutting expenses—it's about cutting the *right* ones.

## CASE STUDY: JAMES & EMILY LOWERY

*Financial freedom ages: 27 & 28*

In 2017, James and Emily Lowery were earning a combined $95,000 a year, but they were essentially living paycheck to paycheck. Their net worth hovered around zero, weighed down by an underwater condo. That same year, James stumbled across the concept of financial independence, and suddenly, everything clicked.

They sat down together, faced their numbers honestly, and began tracking every expense. In James's words, "We didn't just budget—we watched every dollar. That awareness gave us power." Seeing where their money was actually going became the turning point that helped them build a completely different life.

As they tracked their spending, patterns emerged—especially how much was slipping away on defaults and conveniences. In 2017, their monthly spending included:

- $1,400 on housing

- $700 on food

- $500 on transportation

- $500 on entertainment

- $300 on travel

Once they had full visibility into their finances, they began cutting ruthlessly and intentionally.

They bought a duplex and rented out the other unit to eliminate housing costs entirely. They halved their transportation costs when they sold one of the vehicles they barely used. They adopted a simple rule: "If Aldi doesn't carry it, then we can't afford it", and brought their food budget down to $250 a month. Entertainment dropped from $500 to $200. Tracking didn't just show them where the money was going; it showed them exactly where to pull the levers. Their monthly expenses went from $3,400 to $950 in two years.

As their expenses fell, their savings rate skyrocketed. Their income grew year over year, and the gap between income and spending widened dramatically. By 2018, their monthly take-home pay from their jobs reached $6,982, supplemented by $1,790 from rental properties and $500 from side hustles. By 2019, rental income alone exceeded $3,250 a month, which fully covered the cost of their lifestyle.

James and Emily reached financial independence at just 28 and 27 years old. Today, they spend their time traveling slowly, prioritizing health, and taking on projects because they choose to, not because they have to. Looking back, James says the biggest breakthrough came from something simple: getting clear on where their money was actually going. That single habit—tracking every expense—became the catalyst that transformed their finances, their options, and ultimately, their entire lifestyle.

## Call to Action: Track Your Spending

Once you've identified your major spending buckets and your top ten values, track your expenses for the next thirty days. At the end of the month, review each purchase, categorize it, and ask yourself: "Did this align with what I value?" Then adjust your spending accordingly.

If you need an expense-tracking tool, you can find my most up-to-date recommendations here: retireby30book.com/resources

# CHAPTER 4

# MANAGING DEBT

*"There is good debt and bad debt.*
*Good debt is debt that makes you money.*
*Bad debt is debt that costs you money."*

— ROBERT KIYOSAKI

Surveys estimate that over 80% of American households carry some form of debt, so you'd actually be in the minority if you don't have any. Having debt does not mean you've failed. It doesn't make you bad with money, irresponsible, or permanently doomed. It simply means you're human, and that you need a plan to manage it.

A lot of people discover the concept of financial independence *after* they've already accumulated debt. Whether that debt is in the form of credit cards, student loans, or car loans—or all of the above—many people who eventually reach FI start their journey with a negative net worth. Early in my own journey, back in 2018, I had more credit card debt than dollars in my bank account. It wasn't a great feeling.

Debt can feel heavy. It creates stress, guilt, and even avoidance. Some people stop opening statements. Others pretend balances don't exist. I get it. But debt isn't a moral issue. It's a math problem. And math problems can be solved.

The goal of this chapter isn't to shame you or tell you that you must be debt-free before you can move forward. The goal is to help you understand which debt actually needs your attention, which debt can wait, and how to build a simple, repeatable plan to deal with it, without derailing your progress toward financial independence.

## Not All Debt Is Created Equal

One of the biggest mistakes people make with debt is treating it all the same. They lump everything together and feel like they need to attack *every* balance with equal urgency. That usually leads to overwhelm—or worse, doing nothing at all.

A much more useful way to think about debt is through the lens of interest rates. High-interest debt is the real enemy, which typically includes credit card debt and personal loans. When you're paying 15%, 20%, or even 25% interest, that debt is actively working against you every single month. It compounds in the wrong direction. No investment strategy, side hustle, or budgeting trick will reliably outpace that kind of interest. High-interest debt deserves your immediate attention.

Low-interest debt is different. Think mortgages, federal student loans, or auto loans with reasonable rates. These don't usually require the same level of urgency. In many cases, the interest rate is low enough that you *can* make progress toward financial independence while carrying the debt, especially if your cash flow is strong and the debt fits into a broader plan.

This distinction matters because it helps you prioritize. High-interest debt is a fire that needs to be put out. Low-interest debt is more like a slow leak. You don't want to ignore it forever, but you also don't need to panic. Once you understand which balances are actually holding you back, you can focus your energy where it will have the biggest impact, and stop wasting mental bandwidth worrying about debt that doesn't need to be dealt with immediately.

## Credit Cards: Tool or Trap?

Credit cards aren't inherently good or bad—they're just a tool. Like most tools, they can either help you build something useful or cause serious damage if misused. At their core, credit cards are simply a short-term loan. Every time you swipe, you're borrowing money from the bank. If you pay that balance off in full by the due date, you don't pay any interest. If you don't, the interest starts piling up fast. That's where people get into trouble.

The biggest rule with credit cards is simple: if you can't pay your balance in full every month, you shouldn't be using them. At interest rates north of 20%, carrying a balance makes it almost impossible to get ahead. No rewards points or cash back will ever outweigh that kind of interest working against you.

That said, when used responsibly, credit cards can actually be incredibly useful. They offer better fraud protection than debit cards, added purchase protections, and in many cases, travel rewards or cash back on money you were going to spend anyway. I've personally flown around the world using points earned from everyday spending.

Another common misconception is that you need to "carry a balance" to build credit. Carrying a balance just means not paying off your full statement and letting interest accrue into the next month. You don't need to do that. Paying your card off in full every month builds credit without costing you anything. Carrying a balance only benefits the credit card company, not you.

If you currently have credit card debt, that doesn't mean your dreams of financial independence are screwed. It just means this is where your focus should be right now. Pause the rewards game. Stop opening new cards. Get the balance paid down. Once you're consistently paying off your statement balance in full every month, credit cards can re-enter your life as a tool instead of a liability.

## Should You Pay Off Debt or Invest?

We won't dive into investing until later in this book, but I want to address this question now since I've been asked it so many times: *Should I focus on paying off debt first, or should I invest at the same time?* The frustrating answer is—it depends. The good news is that the decision doesn't have to be complicated.

I like to use a 10% interest rate as my benchmark. If the interest rate is above that, I consider it high-interest debt. If it's below that, it falls into the low-interest category.

With high-interest debt, the priority is clear: eliminate it as quickly as possible. This kind of debt is actively working against your financial independence goals, and it's extremely difficult for investments to reliably outpace those interest rates. Paying down debt is a guaranteed return. If you're paying off a credit card with a 25% interest rate, that's the equivalent of locking in a risk-free 25% return (which is incredibly good).

Low-interest debt is a different story. If you have a mortgage or student loans at 3–5%, the math becomes less clear-cut. Historically, the stock market and other proven investments have returned more than that over long periods of time. In situations like these, it can make sense to invest while slowly paying down the debt—especially if doing so improves cash flow, helps you build long-term habits, and keeps you motivated.

But this isn't just a math problem—it's also a behavioral one. Some people sleep better at night knowing they're debt-free.

Others feel more motivated watching their investments grow. Neither approach is wrong. The "best" strategy is the one that helps you stay consistent and avoid burnout.

For many people, a balanced approach works well. High-interest debt gets attacked aggressively, while low-interest debt is paid down more gradually as you continue investing. This allows you to make progress on both fronts without feeling stuck in neutral.

## Debt Payoff Strategies

At this point, you've likely decided that debt payoff should be a priority, but the next question is *how* to actually do it. There are two popular strategies you'll hear about over and over again: the avalanche method and the snowball method.

To best illustrate each of these strategies, let's look at some example debts.

| Debt | Balance | Interest Rate |
|---|---|---|
| Credit Card A | $3,000 | 18% |
| Credit Card B | $6,000 | 25% |
| Student Loan | $12,000 | 4% |
| Car Loan | $18,000 | 6% |

The avalanche method is the math-first approach. You list all your debts by interest rate and aggressively pay down the one with the highest interest first, while making minimum payments on the rest. Once that debt is gone, you move to the next highest interest rate. From a pure numbers standpoint, this approach will save you the most money in interest over time.

| Order | Debt Targeted | Why |
| --- | --- | --- |
| 1 | Credit Card B (25%) | Highest interest |
| 2 | Credit Card A (18%) | Next highest interest |
| 3 | Car Loan (6%) | Lower interest |
| 4 | Student Loan (4%) | Lowest interest |

The snowball method flips that logic. Instead of interest rates, you focus on balances. You pay off your smallest debt first, then roll that payment into the next smallest balance, and so on. This method isn't optimal mathematically, but it can be incredibly effective psychologically. Knocking out small wins early builds momentum and confidence—and for many people, that matters more than saving a few extra dollars in interest.

| Order | Debt Targeted | Why |
| --- | --- | --- |
| 1 | Credit Card B ($3,000) | Smallest balance = quick win |
| 2 | Credit Card A ($6,000) | Momentum builds |
| 3 | Student Loan ($12,000) | Almost there! |
| 4 | Car Loan ($18,000) | Last remaining debt |

The best strategy is the one you'll actually stick with. If seeing quick wins keeps you motivated, the snowball method might be the better fit. If you're disciplined and motivated by efficiency, the avalanche method probably makes more sense.

You can also blend the two. Some people knock out one or two small balances first to build momentum, then switch to the avalanche method to finish strong. Others prioritize any debt above a certain interest rate (say 10%) and ignore balance size altogether. That's perfectly fine.

The most important thing isn't the method you choose—it's that you choose *something* and stick with it. Debt payoff works best when it's systematic and boring. Automate your minimum payments, decide where your extra money is going, and let consistency do the heavy lifting. Over time, those balances will shrink, your cash flow will improve, and progress will start to feel inevitable.

## Debt Freedom Isn't Necessary

You don't have to be completely debt-free to build wealth or reach financial independence. Some types of debt don't require urgency—and in certain cases, paying them off aggressively can actually slow you down.

Mortgages are the most common example. If you have a fixed-rate mortgage at a low interest rate, there's usually no rush to pay it off early. In many cases, that money can be put to better use elsewhere—investing, building an emergency fund, or increasing flexibility in your life. A mortgage is also tied to a real asset that has historically held or grown in value over time.

The same logic often applies to student loans with low interest rates. If your loans are under 10%, you don't need to treat them like an emergency. You can make consistent payments, stay on track, and invest at the same time. For many people, this approach leads to a higher net worth in the long run, even if it takes longer to officially be "debt-free."

If you have a $300,000 mortgage and $100,000 in student loans, it would be unreasonable for me to say you *must* pay off all your debt before starting your FI journey. That could take years—if not decades—before you even reach the starting line. Instead, debt can simply become part of your plan. The goal is to build a payoff strategy that fits your situation, not someone else's rules.

My wife, Lauren, graduated from college with nearly $24,000 in student loans. She didn't wait to start investing or implementing the strategies in this book until every dollar was paid off. She did both in tandem—and that decision helped accelerate our path to financial independence. If you want to eliminate all debt before investing, that's your choice. But in my opinion, debt freedom doesn't need to be the starting point for financial independence. With the right system in place, you can get things moving much sooner.

## Automate Your Debt Payoff

As you'll learn throughout this book, systems beat willpower. Debt payoff is no different. Motivation comes and goes, but systems quietly do the work in the background—whether you're feeling fired up or completely burnt out.

Start by automating the basics. Set all of your minimum payments on autopay so you never miss one. This protects your credit score and removes mental overhead. From there, decide where any *extra* money is going each month. That might be the highest-interest debt (avalanche), the smallest balance (snowball), or a mix of both—but make the decision once and stick to it.

One simple system I like is separating your debt payoff into two buckets:

- Minimums – automated, boring, and non-negotiable

- Extra payments – intentional and targeted

Every month, any extra cash—raises, bonuses, side hustle income, or money left over from under-spending—gets funneled into that second bucket and applied to your high-interest debt. When one loan disappears, roll that payment into the next one. This is how momentum builds.

Before long, you'll find yourself free of high-interest debt, and the money that used to go toward those payments will be freed up for investing, bringing you one step closer to financial independence. Managing debt is just one piece of the expense equation, though. There are much bigger levers you can pull to dramatically reduce your monthly spending, and that's what we'll cover next.

## Call to Action: Create Your Debt Plan

List out every debt you have, including the balance, interest rate, and minimum payment. Decide which payoff strategy you'll use (avalanche, snowball, or a hybrid), then set up autopay for all minimums.

Finally, choose one debt where all extra money will go each month—and commit to it.

# CHAPTER 5

# THE "BIG 3"

*"If you will live like no one else now, later you can live like no one else."*

— DAVE RAMSEY

Growing up, my mom called herself the "coupon queen". She would spend hours cutting coupons, driving to different stores, and buying random items in bulk, just to save something like $17.41. I'm not here to hate on couponing (sorry, Mom), but rather to explain that there are *much* better ways to cut down on your monthly expenses.

That's where "The Big 3" come in: housing, transportation, and food. These three categories make up the majority of the average person's annual spending. According to the Bureau of Labor Statistics, housing, transportation, and food combined can account for almost 65% of a household's annual expenses. That means even small shifts in these areas can lead to thousands in annual savings.

In this chapter, we'll break down each one, show you real-world strategies (and examples from people who've already achieved FI), and help you rethink what's possible with your largest line items. If you get these right, everything else becomes easier. You don't need to stress over lattes or obsess about every little expense. Just optimize the Big 3 and watch the gap between your income and expenses grow.

And remember, these sacrifices are *temporary*. Once you reach financial freedom and beyond, you can start to upgrade your lifestyle again. But in the beginning, maximizing your gap and investing as much as possible are crucial.

## Housing

Housing is the single biggest line item in most people's budgets—often 30–40% of their monthly income. It's also one of the line items that people are least willing to change. I'll admit, reducing this expense does take some effort and sacrifice, but it's one of the best ways to increase your gap.

Let's walk through a few of the best strategies for reducing your housing costs.

### House Hacking

This is one of the most powerful cost-saving strategies out there. House hacking is when you buy a property, live in part of it, and rent out the rest. Maybe it's roommates in a single-family home, or a multi-family property where you live in one unit and rent the other(s). Either way, house hacking can reduce your monthly housing expenses drastically, or in some cases, even convert your housing *expense* into housing *income*.

My friend Craig Curelop, author of *The House Hacking Strategy*, bought a property, rented out all of the bedrooms, and slept on the couch. Extreme? Absolutely. But instead of paying for housing each month, he was making $800 in rental income after all expenses were paid.

Don't worry, you don't have to go as crazy as Craig, but the option is available. When I started looking for my first property, I was tempted to follow in Craig's footsteps, but my wife Lauren told me, "Absolutely not".

So instead, we decided to buy a 3-unit property, live in one of the units, and rent out the other two. Our housing expense turned into $500+ of housing income each month. Compare this to someone paying $1,500 per month for housing. That's a $2,000 difference. Massive.

Now you might be thinking: "If real estate is such a good investment, why don't I just buy a rental property and stay where I am?" Great question. One of the reasons house hacking is so popular is that living in the property allows for much smaller down payments. As an owner-occupant, you can put as little as 3.5% down. If you're buying a rental property you don't plan to live in, expect to need at least 20% down. For a $400,000 house, that's $14,000 down as a house hack, versus $80,000 down as a non-owner-occupied property. I'm ignoring things like closing costs in this example for simplicity, but you get the point.

Not sure where to start? Here are a few types of properties worth exploring:

- Single-family homes (ideal for roommate-style house hacking)

- Accessory Dwelling Units (ADUs) (a basement or garage apartment to offset expenses)

- Duplexes, triplexes, and fourplexes (great for renting out the other units)

We'll cover the real estate buying process later in this book.

## Getting Creative

The average person is spending one-third of their income on housing alone. If you're living paycheck to paycheck, or worse, it might be time to consider downgrading your housing while you kickstart your wealth-building journey. I know this probably isn't what you want to hear, but it's a powerful step to take.

So many personal finance "gurus" out there love to tell you how the secret to saving money is cutting out the lattes, or using apps to find coupons, or other simple tricks to save a buck here or there. But the real change comes from doing uncomfortable things.

It's not easy to give up the nice apartment in the city to move back home for a few years. It's not easy to downsize from a 3-bedroom to a 2-bedroom. It's not easy to have roommates, especially after living on your own. None of this stuff is easy or comfortable, but if it were, everybody would do it. If you want to retire early—like, really early—these are the sacrifices you'll have to make.

Before I saved up the money to buy my first house hack, I lived in an apartment in Boston. A lot of my friends had moved to Boston, and I wanted to experience city living for a bit. The problem was that some of my friends were paying $2,000+ per month in rent for a 1-bedroom apartment. No thanks.

Instead of getting discouraged, though, I got creative. After a bit of searching, three college friends and I found a three-bedroom apartment on the edge of the city listed for $2,700/month. Three bedrooms and four guys. Any guesses on who shared a room? The guy writing a personal finance book, of course.

We split the rent by bedroom, which meant $900 for each room, and since I was sharing, my rent was only $450. It wasn't glamorous, but I was able to save so much more each month.

After college, but before moving to Boston, I moved back into my mom's house for 7 months, despite having an $80,000 corporate finance job where I could have easily gotten my own apartment. Though I was jealous of my friends living on their own, I was saving 80 percent of my income. Definitely worth it.

The reason I'm sharing these stories isn't to convince you to share a small apartment bedroom, or move in with your family—but hey, go for either one of them if you can. Rather, I want to start getting you to think creatively about how you can reduce your housing costs. As I mentioned before, it might not be comfortable, it might not be sexy, but it will be worth it in the long run.

## Transportation

Transportation is the second-highest spending category for most people. The average American spends around 17% of their annual budget on cars, gas, insurance, and maintenance. It's also another category that's not exactly *easy* to change, but the benefits are well worth it.

First rule: Never lease a car. Leasing is a bad financial decision for 99.9% of people. You're essentially renting a depreciating asset while paying top dollar. At the end of your lease, you own nothing. And yes, even most lease-to-own agreements are a ripoff.

Second rule: Avoid buying new. Cars lose 20–30% of their value the second you drive them off the lot. Buying a used car means someone else already took the depreciation hit. Every dealership will try to lure you into buying new with lots of "amazing" perks and guarantees, but it's rarely worth it.

The smartest move is to buy a 5-7 year old used car. Something affordable, but reliable. Have it checked out by a mechanic before you buy. If possible, avoid financing it. No car payment.

No stress. Just cheap, dependable transportation that gets you where you need to go. Despite reaching financial freedom, I still drive the same 2015 Nissan Frontier to this day.

Not only does driving a boring, paid-off car save you money—it saves you *decisions*. No worrying about payments, upgrades, or trade-ins. It's one less thing cluttering your mind.

Public transportation, biking, walking, and carpooling are all viable options, too, depending on your location. I know people who sold their second car, moved closer to work, or even went car-free, and saved thousands in the process.

This doesn't mean you can't ever enjoy a nice car, but that decision should come *after* you've built a strong financial base, not before.

## Food

The third member of the Big 3 is food. Between groceries, takeout, and dining out, the average household spends 11–13% of its income here. And it's one of the easiest categories to spiral out of control if you're not paying attention.

So what works?

- Make a grocery list—and stick to it. You'll save money and avoid impulse buys.

- Plan your meals. Even a loose plan for the week can prevent midweek "what's for dinner?" takeout decisions.

- Limit eating out. You don't need to cut it completely, but set a budget and stick to it.

Deprivation is not the goal here. Please don't cut out all the fun in your life in the name of saving money. During the most frugal years of my FI journey, I'd still go out with my friends multiple times per week. I just made a few conscious tweaks to make things more affordable.

Sometimes my wife and I would share one big entree, instead of ordering multiple and having leftovers—which happens all too often. Other times, when our friends were heading out to the bar, we'd pre-game at the house and only order a drink or two out. We weren't missing out on the experience, just spending more intentionally.

If you're trying to cut back on spending without skipping social events, try hosting a potluck, picnic, or barbecue. Most people go out to eat for the social experience, and they'd be just as happy with a home-cooked meal, which costs a lot less.

At the end of the day, this isn't a category that I recommend cutting to the bare minimum. You don't need to eat rice and beans to reach financial independence. You can buy quality, healthy foods to cook at home, spend consciously at restaurants, and find creative ways to get social.

## What If My Big 3 Are Different?

While housing, transportation, and food are the Big 3 for the average person, I understand that some people's expense categories might look different. Maybe it's daycare, student loans, insurance, credit card debt, or travel that make up a larger slice of the pie, and that's fine.

No matter what your Big 3 are, the point of this chapter is to help you identify them and figure out creative ways to reduce them. One of *the* most important traits among all of the early retirees I've met is creativity. Those who learn ways to beat the status quo, win.

If you're worried about what others might think of the changes you're making, consider this: A house hacker could be living right next door, and you'd never know. A 7-year-old car still looks and runs great. And splitting an entrée? Totally normal. Throw in an appetizer if you're feeling wild. The real difference isn't what people see. It's the thousands of dollars you're saving behind the scenes each month that will launch you toward financial independence.

If you've heard of the 80/20 Principle, also known as the Pareto Principle, it states that roughly 80% of outcomes come from 20% of inputs. In the context of this chapter, that means a few key expense categories drive most of your spending. Focus on optimizing those, and don't waste energy sweating the small stuff.

## A Temporary Trade-Off

If any of this feels like you're "roughing it," remember: it's temporary. The FI lifestyle isn't about cutting forever. It's about cutting back *now* so you can buy your freedom *later*.

House hacking, driving an older car, cooking at home—it may not feel Instagram-worthy, but it's how countless early retirees made it work. Saving a dollar here and there isn't how people retire in their 20s, 30s, and 40s. It's minimizing their Big 3, creating a huge savings gap, and investing the difference.

If you remember the chart I shared in Chapter 1, the more aggressively you save now, the quicker you'll reach financial independence. In the *Investing* section of this book, you'll learn about the power of compound interest and why having a high savings rate—especially during the early years—is so important.

Since I've reached FI, I've upgraded my lifestyle significantly. We're in the process of building our dream house, we travel without a budget, and dine out multiple times per week without having to look at the bill. But none of this would have been possible if we hadn't ruthlessly cut our Big 3 during the early years of our FI journey.

When you're financially independent, you can choose how you spend your money. But until then, choose to spend it wisely.

## A Look Into the Numbers

To give you an idea of just how powerful optimizing the Big 3 can be, let's look at a case study. Derek and Kayla are neighbors who both live in the suburbs of Chicago. Derek rents a two-bedroom apartment in a duplex for $1,650 per month. Kayla lives next door, in a near-identical duplex, but instead of renting, she bought the place and decided to rent out the other unit. Her all-in housing expenses (mortgage, interest, maintenance, etc.) would be $2,250 per month, but since she rents out the other unit for $1,500, she only pays $750 out of pocket.

Last year, Derek bought a brand new car that came with a $600-per-month payment. After accounting for insurance, gas, and maintenance, he averages $850 per month. Kayla, on the other hand, drives a 7-year-old car that she paid off and spends only $300 each month.

Kayla cooks at home most nights, but goes out or grabs takeout once or twice per week. When she does go out, she'll usually share an entree with a friend, and maybe an appetizer too. Derek, on the other hand, is always scrambling at meal time, so he's constantly getting food delivered. On his nights out, he orders multiple drinks, an app, an entree, and maybe a dessert. In an average month, Kayla spends $400, and Derek spends $650 on food.

From the outside, their lives don't look all that different, but when it comes to the numbers, the difference is shocking.

|  | **Derek** | **Kayla** |
| --- | --- | --- |
| Housing | $1,650 | $750 |
| Transportation | $850 | $300 |
| Food | $650 | $400 |
| Total | $3,150 | $1,450 |

Derek is spending more than *double* what Kayla is spending on the Big 3 each month—a $1,700 difference. That's $20,400 per year. Or $204,000 over a decade.

## Call to Action: Tackle the Big 3

I'm sure you've had thoughts and ideas about the Big 3 in the back of your mind throughout this chapter, but unless you make a plan to take concrete steps, it's all just empty intentions. And intentions alone don't get you any closer to early retirement. Choose at least one Big 3 category and take action:

- Try house hacking or downgrading to cut housing costs
- Swap your leased or new car for something reliable and fully paid off
- Prep meals at home this week instead of ordering out

The faster you adjust your Big 3, the closer you'll be to early retirement.

# CHAPTER 6

# 20 WAYS TO SAVE MONEY

*"A penny saved is a penny earned."*

— Benjamin Franklin

If you've made it this far, you've already started to build the muscle of intentionality. You've tracked your expenses, you understand where your money is going, and you've tackled the Big 3. Now let's go even deeper.

This chapter is your tactical toolkit—your menu of smart, effective, real-world ways to cut costs without sacrificing your lifestyle. Some of these will save you hundreds, and others, just a few bucks. But together they'll accelerate your savings rate and bring you one step closer to financial independence.

Pick a few to start with. Experiment. See what sticks. You don't have to do everything, but every intentional choice you make is a step toward more freedom.

Let's dive into the list.

## Big Wins & Monthly Bills

These tips target recurring expenses—the big stuff that moves the needle.

### 1. Automate Your Savings

Set up automatic transfers from checking to savings or investment accounts. You won't miss what you never see— and it removes the mental friction of deciding whether to save each month. Even $100 per month adds up to $1,200 per year. Treat saving like a bill you can't skip.

### 2. Refinance High-Interest Debt

Drop your interest rate on student loans, credit cards, or personal loans to save hundreds or thousands over time. Start by reviewing your loan terms and comparing them with offers from other banks or lenders. Focus on credit cards over 15% APR or loans above 6–7%. Refinancing makes the biggest difference if you have solid credit and a few years left on the payoff timeline.

### 3. Optimize Your Insurance

Combine home, auto, or renters insurance with the same provider and ask for a multi-policy discount. Requote your insurance every 6–12 months by comparing offers from multiple providers or calling a few local agents directly. Here's a simple script to get started:

> *"Hi, I'm reviewing my expenses and noticed my premium is higher than some competitors. Are there any discounts or options to lower my rate while keeping similar coverage?"*

Then, call two competitors and say:

> *"I'm currently paying $X/month for auto/home coverage. Can you offer me a better deal for equivalent protection?"*

You don't have to be aggressive—just curious and clear. Most reps are used to this question.

## 4. Downgrade Your TV & Internet

Take a closer look at your TV and internet bills—are you really using all the features you're paying for? You could save up to $100 a month just by downsizing your cable package. Consider ditching cable altogether, canceling unused streaming or premium subscriptions, or switching to a lower-cost internet plan.

## 5. Switch to a Cheaper Cell Phone Plan

Many people don't realize this, but there are now dozens of low-cost cell phone carriers that use the exact same towers as the major providers. The difference is that one plan might cost you $15 a month, while another charges $100 for essentially the same service. The best part is that you can customize your plan to fit your needs.

## 6. Leverage Family Plans and Sharing Economies

Split memberships, phone plans, streaming accounts, and more to slash monthly costs. I have a family cell phone plan, multiple shared streaming accounts, a shared gym membership, and even a family Duolingo plan for learning Spanish.

## 7. Cancel Auto-Renew by Default

Subscriptions are designed to be forgotten. Turn off auto-renewal the moment you sign up for something. It forces you to re-evaluate if it's worth keeping—and prevents years of mindless charges for services you no longer use.

## Everyday Spending Habits

These are daily decisions that add up fast.

## 8. Use a Grocery List and Shop Strategically

Impulse purchases can derail your food budget fast. You've probably heard the advice, 'Never go to the grocery store hungry'—and it's true. You'll save money each week just by sticking to a list and avoiding those midweek 'just one thing' trips. And waste less food, too. Grocery shopping via app is a great option as well since you can find in-app coupons, compare prices quickly, and avoid seeing or smelling something "too good" to pass up.

## 9. Meal Prep

You don't need to become a full-blown meal prepper. Just planning a few meals in advance or doubling your dinner portions can dramatically reduce how often you grab takeout. Back when I was living on $25–30 a week for groceries, this was my go-to strategy. It took a little extra effort, but it saved me hundreds each month and eliminated the "what's for dinner" stress.

## 10. Use Cash for Discretionary Spending

Withdraw your "fun money" in cash. Once it's gone, you're done spending for the week. Set a weekly cash limit for dining out, shopping, or entertainment, and keep it in a separate envelope or wallet. It helps you feel the transaction and creates a hard limit that swiping a card can't match.

## 11. Delay Big Purchases (Then Decide)

Impulse spending adds up fast. By waiting 48 hours before buying anything over $100, you create space to decide if the purchase actually adds value to your life. I've dodged dozens of regrettable purchases this way. Plus, the delay gives you time to look for a discount or a used version instead. In some cases, websites will even offer deals on items left sitting in your cart.

## 12. Do a 30-Day Spending Detox

Pick a category—Amazon, takeout, Target runs—and cut it out completely for 30 days. No cheating. The purchase can wait. It's a powerful reset that helps you see what you actually miss (if anything) and what you were just buying on autopilot.

## Lifestyle Hacks & Mindset Shifts

Creative or mindset-based savings strategies that make frugality feel intentional.

### 13. Buy Used Whenever Possible

Furniture, clothes, gear—you name it. Nearly everything you need is already out there in great condition at half the price. There are plenty of hidden gems on places like Facebook Marketplace and eBay.

### 14. Tap Into Free Local Resources

Free fitness classes, coworking rooms, tools, and events are often available through community centers and public libraries. Books, audiobooks, movies, language courses, and more are all free with a library card. You can get all your favorite books for free with apps like Libby and Hoopla.

### 15. Travel Smarter with Rewards and Alternatives

Travel doesn't have to break the bank. I've flown across the world on airline miles and stayed in Airbnbs for half the price of a hotel. I have friends who score free lodging through house swaps or house-sitting gigs. If you're willing to look beyond the typical 7-day, all-inclusive resort vacation, there are plenty of ways to scratch your travel itch without spending a small fortune.

### 16. Set Up Money Dates (Solo or with a Partner)

Review your spending weekly or monthly and make sure it matches your goals. My wife and I sit down at the end of each month to go over our finances and make adjustments when we need to. Having someone in your corner who shares your goals is a superpower on the path to financial freedom, and it becomes infinitely easier when you both know the numbers.

### 17. Go DIY (Within Reason)

You don't need to know how to fix everything, but learning how to patch drywall, change your oil, or troubleshoot small repairs can save thousands over time. YouTube has a tutorial for everything, and confidence grows with every task you tackle.

### 18. Ask for the Discount

Call your service providers or ask in-store—you'd be surprised how often it works. I've gotten credit card annual fees waived, $200 in-store discounts, and full refunds just by asking politely. The worst they can say is "no".

### 19. Make "Fun" a Line Item

Budgeting isn't about restriction. It's about permission. When you set aside money specifically for fun, it helps you enjoy life without guilt or overspending. Whether it's $100/month for concerts or spontaneous weekend trips, knowing your limit creates freedom within structure. The best budget is the one you're most likely to follow.

## 20. Avoid Lifestyle Inflation

As your income grows, it's tempting to upgrade everything—your apartment, your car, your habits. But raises don't have to turn into higher spending. By keeping your expenses mostly the same and intentionally directing new income toward savings or investments, you dramatically increase your savings rate. This is one of the fastest ways to accelerate your path to financial independence, without feeling deprived.

## Frugal vs. Cheap

There's a fine line between being frugal and being cheap, and it's one that's easy to cross if you're not careful. Being frugal means spending with intention. Being cheap often means sacrificing quality, relationships, or joy.

| Frugal | Cheap |
|---|---|
| Packing a lunch for work | Stiffing the server on a tip |
| Buying a reliable, used car | Skipping oil changes to save money |
| Suggesting a potluck vs. a dinner out | "Forgetting" your wallet at a group dinner |

You don't need to pinch every penny. You just need to make sure each dollar you spend aligns with your values. Frugality is about focusing on long-term value, not just short-term cost. Some people take saving to an extreme and cross the line into being cheap, and that's not what I'm promoting here.

Spend with intention, be generous, and don't compromise your values just to save a few dollars. What you put out into the world has a way of coming back around. When you're unsure whether a choice is frugal or cheap, ask yourself: 'Does this decision negatively impact someone else?' If the answer is yes, you're probably being cheap.

## The Expense Floor

This section of the book has focused on cutting expenses, and that's intentional. It's often the easiest place to start when you're trying to widen the gap between what you earn and what you spend. But there's a limit to how much you can cut. Eventually, you hit the floor.

You need a place to live, food to eat, and basic health care. If your expenses are already trimmed to the essentials, there's only so much farther you can go without sacrificing your well-being. Could you live in a cardboard box and scavenge for food, and reach a 100% savings rate? Sure. But obviously, that's not the goal. Financial independence shouldn't come at the cost of your health or happiness.

If you found yourself shaking your head during the last few chapters, thinking there's no way to cut your expenses any further, you're going to love this next section. Especially for low earners, increasing your income is the most powerful way to grow the gap.

Everyone has a different expense floor depending on where they live, but if your income is at or below the poverty line in your area, cutting costs alone won't be enough. At that point, boosting your income isn't optional—it's essential. Buckle up.

## CASE STUDY: JESSE RAY

*Financial freedom age: 28*

Jesse Ray's journey to financial independence didn't start with a high salary or a lucky break. It started with learning how to live on almost nothing. From a young age, his parents taught him delayed gratification. If he wanted something, they'd sit him down and help him map out exactly how much he needed to earn before he could buy it. That habit of being intentional with every dollar became the foundation for the way he approached money as an adult.

When Jesse graduated from college and entered the workforce, he wasn't earning much—just $2,200 a month in 2016. But instead of trying to "look successful," he focused on keeping his expenses as low as possible. He rarely spent more than $1,000 a month during those early years. He lived with roommates, drove an older car, limited his discretionary spending, and questioned every expense. Groceries, transportation, entertainment—everything was stripped down to the essentials. What he lacked in income at the beginning, he made up for with relentless discipline.

As his income grew through his sales career, Jesse held firm. While many people increase their spending as they earn more, Jesse resisted lifestyle inflation at every turn. Even in 2021, when he was bringing in over $12,000 per month, his budget was still intentionally lean. He lived in a modest apartment, spent $300 on groceries, $350 on eating out, $200 on gas, and $20 on a gym membership. He didn't chase upgrades or splurges. He continued driving his Honda Civic, avoided unnecessary subscriptions, and looked for creative ways to keep expenses as low as possible.

The massive gap Jesse created between his income and expenses allowed him to invest aggressively in both the stock market and real estate. While his peers succumbed to lifestyle inflation, Jesse remained frugal and put his extra dollars to work.  He quickly built his stock portfolio to $100,000 and bought rental properties that produced thousands in monthly cash flow. After just a few years of disciplined saving and investing, work became optional.

Jesse reached financial independence at 28 years old, and today he channels his time into building communities for entrepreneurs and athletes. He credits the speed of his journey to keeping his expenses low and refusing to give in to lifestyle pressure. While friends upgraded their apartments, bought new cars, and spent weekends "living it up," Jesse stayed focused on his long-term vision. That discipline is what allowed him to build wealth at such a rapid pace.

## Call to Action: Try One This Week

Pick *at least* one savings strategy from this chapter and implement it in the next seven days. Maybe it's calling your insurance company. Maybe it's switching phone plans or using cash for eating out. Whatever it is, put it into motion.

For an updated list of my favorite cost-saving tools and websites, visit retireby30book.com/resources.

# SECTION 3

# INCOME

# CHAPTER 7

# SIDE HUSTLES

*"You don't learn to walk by following rules. You learn
by doing, and by falling over."*

— RICHARD BRANSON

I'll admit—I'm a bit biased when it comes to side hustles. They're the reason I was able to quit my corporate job after just seven months, save over 80% of my income, and reach financial independence in only three years. But I've learned a lot since those early days.

To give you an idea, here's a "short" list of side hustles I've tried:

- selling digital products

- landscaping

- tutoring

- podcasting

- flipping stuff on eBay
- managing rental properties
- blogging
- social media influencer
- creating a custom clothing line
- running Airbnbs
- manufacturing disc golf equipment
- running a course-building agency
- baling Christmas trees
- freelance writing
- delivering Uber Eats on a bike
- editing podcasts
- petsitting
- building websites
- waiting tables
- email marketing
- teacher's assistant
- house flipping
- video editing
- money coaching
- managing affiliate programs
- buffing boats
- planning a book tour

Some of my side hustles were terrible, some were decent, and a few have stuck with me to this day. But every single one taught me something. If you're new to side hustling, experiment early and often. You won't know what you enjoy, or what you're good at, until you try a bunch of things. At one point, I had 19 side hustles going at once (way too many), but that season helped me quickly learn what I liked, what I didn't, and what actually worked for me.

People often ask, "What's the best side hustle?" That's like asking, "What's the best food?" There's no right answer. It depends entirely on you, your skills, and your interests. For me, experimenting was the key, and I'd encourage you to take the same approach. My financial life was completely transformed in just a few short years, and your future self will thank you for diving into this chapter and starting sooner rather than later.

Side hustling isn't just about earning a little extra cash; it's about taking control of your income and proving that you don't need a boss to make money. Whether you're paying off debt, boosting your savings rate, or working toward a big goal, even a few hundred extra dollars a month can be the game-changer that shifts everything.

## Types of Side Hustles

Side hustles come in many forms, but most fall into four main types, each with different time demands, income potential, and growth paths. Think of these as tools in a toolkit—just pick the one that fits your skills, schedule, and goals.

## *1. Trade Time for Money*

These are straightforward: you do the work, you get paid. They're great for getting started fast, but they're often capped by how many hours you can work.

- **Freelancing** - Offer services like writing, graphic design, web development, or virtual assistance through platforms like Upwork, Fiverr, or your own network.

- **Tutoring or Teaching** - Teach a subject you know well (academic or creative) through platforms like Wyzant, Preply, or locally. This often involves high hourly rates and flexible hours.

- **Delivery Driving** - Work for services like DoorDash, Uber Eats, Instacart, or Amazon Flex. Fast to start, flexible shifts, and income scales with time invested.

- **Babysitting or Pet Sitting** - Use Care.com, Rover, or word-of-mouth to find regular gigs. Great for dependable, repeatable income.

- **Handyman or Yard Work** - Mow lawns, rake leaves, assemble furniture, or do basic repairs. Post locally or on TaskRabbit and Facebook groups.

- **House Cleaning** - Launch solo or through sites like Thumbtack or Craigslist. Recurring clients = recurring income. Benefits include low startup costs and high demand.

- **Rideshare Driving** - Drive for Uber or Lyft. Works well if you already have a car and like flexibility.

- **Event Staffing or Bartending** - Help at weddings, parties, or local events—especially weekends and holidays. Often pays well and doesn't require long-term commitment.

- **Photography Gigs** - Take family portraits, headshots, or real estate photos. Minimal gear needed to start if you're already an amateur photographer, and word-of-mouth can grow this quickly.

- **Flipping Items for Profit** - Buy low and sell high on Facebook Marketplace, Craigslist, eBay, or OfferUp. Requires time to find, fix, or clean up items—but quick to monetize.

When I had lots of free time and energy, the "trade time for money" side hustles were great. I could side hustle for 5 hours after work one day, and take the next day off. There's always more work to do. This category is all about speed and flexibility.

## 2. Build a Scalable Side Hustle

These take more upfront time and effort, but the upside is much bigger. You can earn money while you sleep once the system is in place.

- **Create and Sell Digital Products** - Think ebooks, templates, Notion dashboards, spreadsheets, or planners. Build once, sell forever.

  → *Great for: creatives, educators, and systems-minded folks.*

- **Launch an Online Course** - Teach a skill you know well (design, freelancing, marketing, etc.) on platforms like Teachable, Podia, or Gumroad.

  → *Pairs well with YouTube or a blog to build an audience.*

- **Build a Personal Brand** - Post regularly on social media, create a website, build a following, and monetize with ads, affiliate links, or digital products.

  → *Example: a personal brand about van life, vegan cooking, or DIY tips.*

- **Grow a YouTube Channel** - Create educational, entertaining, or how-to content. Monetize with ad revenue, sponsorships, affiliate links, or product sales.

  → *Longer ramp-up time, but huge earning potential once you build traction.*

- **Open an Etsy or Shopify Store (Digital or Physical)** - Sell your own creations—digital prints, T-shirts, crafts, or handmade goods. With the right systems, fulfillment can be automated.

  → *Example: selling Canva templates, wedding invitations, or custom apparel.*

- **Affiliate Marketing** - Promote tools or products you love and earn a commission on each sale. This works well with blogs, email lists, and YouTube.

  → *The key is building trust and choosing the right niche.*

- **Develop an App or Software Tool** - Have a pain point? Build a lightweight app, plugin, or tool that solves it—and sell access.

  → *More technical, but high recurring revenue potential.*

- **Build a Membership or Subscription Community** - Offer exclusive content, coaching, or resources for a monthly fee. Use platforms like Skool, Circle, or Kajabi.

  → *Great for niche topics and passionate audiences.*

- **Write and Self-Publish a Book** - Write a helpful nonfiction guide or a compelling novel. Sell on Amazon KDP or your own site.

  → *Good for evergreen income with zero ongoing effort once launched.*

- **License Your Work or Intellectual Property** - Create templates, designs, courses, or software you can license to others—agencies, educators, or companies.

  → *One effort, multiple payouts over time.*

Scalable side hustles take longer to ramp up, but they offer time freedom on the other side. Today, I spend almost all of my time in this category between my digital products, online courses, memberships, websites, and social media channels.

### 3. The Sharing Economy

This is all about monetizing assets you already own. If you have something useful and underutilized, someone else is probably willing to pay for access to it.

- **Rent Out a Room** - Turn your spare bedroom (or your whole home when you're away) into income. Some Airbnb and VRBO hosts earn thousands a month with the right setup.

- **Share Your Car** - If you don't drive every day, rent out your vehicle on a site like Turo or Getaround and turn it into a passive asset instead of a depreciating one.

- **Offer Storage Space** - Have an empty garage, basement, or shed? Rent it out to people on a platform like Neighbor who need extra storage—no lifting or logistics involved.

- **House Sit or Rent Your Place While Traveling** - Live rent-free while watching someone's home (and pets), or rent out your place while you're away to offset your own travel costs on sites like TrustedHousesitters.

- **Rent Out Tools or Equipment** - Got a pressure washer, power tools, camera gear, or party supplies? Rent them out locally through Fat Llama, Loanables, or Facebook Marketplace.

- **Share Your Parking Spot or Driveway** - In cities or event-heavy areas, rent your driveway or reserved spot on platforms like SpotHero, JustPark, or even Craigslist.

- **Pet Sit or Dog Board via Rover** - If you already have a pet who gets along with others, what's adding one more into the mix? You can earn money boarding dogs or pet-sitting while their owners are away.

- **List Your Pool, Backyard, or Venue Space** - Platforms like Swimply and Peerspace let you rent out private spaces for events, photoshoots, or casual gatherings.

This type of side hustle is often overlooked, but it can offer some of the highest earnings per hour. My friend and podcast co-host, Justin Taylor, lives in Austin, Texas, and rents out his house during major events like ACL and SXSW. On the busiest weekends, he's booked his place for as much as $800 per night.

You might just be sitting on a goldmine, too.

*4. Hybrid Hustles*

These often start as trading time and evolve into scalable businesses. You earn upfront by doing the work yourself, then gradually build systems, products, or a team that allows you to step back. It's the best of both worlds: quick income now, with the option to create leverage and long-term freedom down the road.

- **Freelance Writing → Content Agency or Productized Service** - Start by writing for clients. Over time, create SOPs, hire subcontractors, and turn it into a streamlined business that runs without your daily involvement.

- **Tutoring → Online Course or Group Program** - Begin with 1:1 tutoring. Once you see what students struggle with most, build a self-paced course or host group sessions to scale your time.

- **Handyman Services → Property Maintenance Business** - Start by doing odd jobs—fixing doors, patching drywall, assembling furniture. Once you've built a reputation, you can hire subcontractors and turn it into a local maintenance business.

- **Virtual Assistant → VA Agency** - Start as a solo VA. As demand grows, hire other VAs and manage the business. You shift from doing the work to overseeing systems.

- **Dog Sitting on Rover → Pet Care Business or Subscription Service** - Begin with pet sitting or dog walking. Build relationships, then offer recurring packages, grooming add-ons, or pet supply subscriptions.

- **Selling on Facebook Marketplace → Flipping Course or Coaching** - Flip furniture or gear locally. Once you've nailed the process, teach others how to do it through an ebook, paid community, or video series.

- **Podcast Editing → Monthly Retainers or Productized Packages** - Start by editing shows for individuals. Over time, offer fixed packages (e.g., 4 episodes/month + show notes) and hand off the editing to a small team.

- **Freelance Design → Template Shop** - Begin with client design work, then turn your most requested work into Canva or Adobe templates you can sell passively.

- **Local Yard Work → Property Maintenance Company** - Start by mowing lawns or shoveling snow. Build a client base, then subcontract the work and focus on scheduling, sales, and marketing.

- **Coaching → Group Coaching or Membership Community** - Begin with 1:1 sessions. As demand grows, create group offerings, live workshops, or a membership site with resources, calls, and a community.

Some people are perfectly happy trading their time for money and never advancing their side hustle to this "hybrid" category, and that's okay! The side hustle(s) you choose are completely up to you and your preferences.

## How to Find the Right Side Hustle for You

The best side hustle is the one you'll actually stick with. Let's recap quickly and take a look at the four main side hustle types.

| Hustle Type | Time to Start | Scalability |
| --- | --- | --- |
| Trade Time for Money | Low | Low |
| Scalable Business | High | High |
| Sharing Economy | Low | Medium |
| Hybrid Hustle | Medium | High |

If you choose to trade your time for money, begin by looking at your existing skill set. What do people frequently ask you for help with? What's something you don't mind doing regularly? This type of side hustle is often the fastest to launch. You could realistically start tomorrow.

Scalable businesses, on the other hand, are more about what you *know*. Knowledge is one of the most scalable assets you can leverage. Is there a topic you're already the go-to person for among friends or family? That expertise could become a course, a digital product, or a content-driven business. While these ventures take longer to ramp up, the income potential on the other side is massive.

The sharing economy is pretty straightforward. It's about using what you already have, and being willing to rent or share it. A spare room, a car, a camera, a pool, or even a set of power tools can become income-producing assets with the right platform and a little creativity. You could start earning real money with this type of hustle within days.

And then there are hybrid side hustles, where time-for-money work evolves into something scalable. If you go this route, document everything as you go: your workflow, communication templates, pricing, and processes. You'll thank yourself later. When it's time to hire help, automate tasks, or productize your services, you'll already have the systems in place to grow into a real business.

No matter which type of side hustle you choose, try to pick something that gives you energy—or at the very least, something you don't dread doing. Sometimes the goal of financial freedom is enough to keep you motivated, but not always. It's much easier to stay consistent with a hustle you don't actively dislike.

You might already be brainstorming your first side hustle ideas, or you might be feeling lost and racking your brain for what skills or knowledge you could possibly sell. The good news is that anything is learnable. Between YouTube, A.I., social media, books, podcasts, courses, and memberships, there's nothing you can't learn.

The skills I have today are *way* different than the skills I started with. And my side hustle graveyard is filled with old projects and business ideas. Your first hustle doesn't have to be your last. Most people don't get it right on the first try.

Action creates clarity. At first, it can feel like throwing spaghetti at the wall, and you'll question if it's worth it. But the people who keep going are the ones who build real freedom. The more things you try, the more patterns you recognize, and the closer you get to something sustainable.

## Side Hustle to Retirement

Let's do some quick math. Let's say you want to earn an extra $1,000 per month. Sounds scary, right? But making an extra $33 today? That sounds doable. And $33 per day over the next month means an extra ~$1,000 in income. Small, consistent steps lead to big outcomes.

I still remember making my first $5 online back in 2018. It wasn't much—but it was the spark that lit a fire. That tiny sale proved I didn't need a boss to make money. I could earn income on my own. Back then, I was pouring every spare minute into my side hustles. I'd wake up at 5:30 a.m., drive to the train station, and work on the train for an hour and a half. Choosing the train instead of driving gave me three additional hours per day to make money outside my 9-to-5.

At work, I'd sneak in side hustle tasks when I could (don't tell my old boss), work on the train ride home, hit the gym, eat dinner, and keep hustling until bed. I was regularly putting in 14 to 16-hour days—driven by the dream of financial freedom and quitting my job. After seven months, that effort paid off. I was earning $1,200 to $1,500 a month consistently from my side hustles: a mix of digital products, blogging, podcasting, and freelancing. It was a blend of time-for-money gigs and scalable projects, and it was enough to change everything.

You can't imagine the doors that open once you take that first step. Did I ever think selling $5 digital products on Etsy would grow into a 7-figure business and a community of over 20,000 people? Absolutely not. But none of it would've been possible if I hadn't put myself out there and just started.

Side hustles can have a massive impact on your path to financial independence. Later in this book, when we dive into investing and compound interest, you'll see just how powerful an extra $100, $500, or $1,000 a month can be. It's not just about the money. You'll also gain skills, confidence, and connections that compound just as powerfully.

For me, side hustling was one of the biggest reasons I reached financial independence by age 25. If you haven't started earning outside your 9–5 yet, I strongly encourage you to give it a shot. But if you're laser-focused on your career, have limited time, and want to boost your income through your day job instead—stick around, because the next chapter is for you.

## CASE STUDY: STEVEN AND LAUREN KEYS

*Financial freedom ages: 29 & 30*

For Steven and Lauren Keys, side hustles weren't just a way to earn extra cash. They were the engine that powered their path to financial independence. From the beginning, they approached income differently than most young teachers. They didn't rely solely on their modest salaries of $35,000 and $38,000. Instead, they constantly looked for ways to earn outside the classroom: freelancing, tutoring, building online projects, and eventually creating their own business. Those small experiments became the bridge between their traditional jobs and the freedom they wanted.

Their background helped shape that mindset. Lauren grew up helping her family run all kinds of micro-businesses, from selling phones at flea markets to assembling real estate mailers. Steven learned steady, practical money habits from his divorced parents. When the two started their careers, they brought those experiences together and immediately began testing new ways to increase their income. What began as small tutoring gigs grew into CramBetter—a college study platform they built themselves. That one side hustle snowballed, eventually generating meaningful income for years.

As they layered in additional freelance work, blog earnings, and seasonal jobs, their combined income began to climb. Some years, their side hustles helped push their monthly earnings to $10,000–$13,000. Because they kept their expenses low—often under $2,000 a month—they were able to save aggressively and gain the confidence to take extended sabbaticals.

Their side hustle income became so reliable that when they eventually hit FI, they didn't have to draw from their investment portfolio at all. Those flexible income streams gave them freedom long before the math said they were "supposed" to retire.

Their financial picture continued to grow as they invested the surplus from both their salaries and their side hustles. By mid-2015, just two years into their careers, they had saved more than $100,000. They invested in index funds, bought a rental property, and treated every new side project as a chance to learn, experiment, and diversify. Their net worth surpassed $153,000 by 2015, exceeded $1 million by 2023, and has since continued climbing, largely because their entrepreneurial efforts covered their lifestyle along the way.

Today, Steven and Lauren live in a paid-off beach condo in St. Augustine, Florida. They spend their time running CramBetter, maintaining their blog Trip of a Lifestyle, and taking on creative projects whenever they feel inspired. Travel, hobbies, painting, gaming, and French lessons—their life is a mix of exploration and purpose. Side hustles didn't just accelerate their journey to FI, they gave them freedom years before they technically reached it.

## Call to Action: Start Your Side Hustle

Don't get stuck brainstorming. Pick one side hustle idea and test it this month. Knock on doors, list something for rent, send a pitch, or launch a mini product. Use your time, skills, or stuff to earn your first dollar—then see where it leads.

For a master list of side hustles, visit retireby30book.com/resources.

# CHAPTER 8

# MAXIMIZING YOUR DAY JOB

*"Your job is not your life. It's a tool. Use it."*

— RYAN HOLIDAY

Of course, I'm a bit biased toward side hustles since that was the path I took, but not everyone wants to quit their job to become a full-time entrepreneur—and you don't have to. For many people on the path to financial independence, your 9–5 can be one of your greatest assets, because increasing your income at your day job is often the fastest, most reliable way to boost your savings rate.

Instead of seeing your job as a barrier to freedom, try seeing it as a launchpad. You can earn more, learn more, and build options. All while still collecting a paycheck.

This approach is especially relevant for high-income earners with strong upside potential—think sales roles, performance-based compensation, or commission-heavy jobs. If you have the opportunity to earn an extra $50,000 just by doubling down at work—without building a side hustle from scratch—that's a no-brainer.

Not sure how to actually increase your income through your day job? Let's dive into some of the most effective strategies to make it happen.

## Negotiate a Raise

If you're delivering results, you should be paid accordingly, but most people never ask. They hope their work "speaks for itself." Unfortunately, silence doesn't pay better. I've seen friends boost their income by $60,000+ simply by asking.

Here's how to position yourself for a raise:

1. **Track your wins.** Keep a running list of accomplishments, KPIs hit, testimonials, and problems solved. Bring them to your next review.

2. **Set expectations early.** At the beginning of the quarter or year, tell your manager what you're aiming for. Ask what success looks like from their point of view.

3. **Practice the ask.** If you don't ask, things likely won't change. Figure out the best way to discuss your compensation when the time comes.

Here are a few sample scripts to choose from:

- "Based on the results I've delivered and the goals we set, I'd like to revisit my compensation. Is this a good time to talk about that?"

- "I've really enjoyed taking on additional responsibilities this quarter, especially [specific project]. I'd love to discuss how my role and compensation could evolve to reflect that impact."

- "I've done some market research, and based on my performance and what I'm seeing in similar roles, I'd like to revisit my compensation. I love working here and hope we can figure something out. Would you be open to discussing that?"

- "I love working here and see myself growing with the company. Can you help me better understand what steps I can take to increase my compensation and responsibility over time? Would you be open to creating a plan together?"

- "If I were to take on a leadership project or contribute outside my role in a measurable way, could we tie that to a performance-based bonus or title adjustment?"

You don't have to use these scripts verbatim, but hopefully, they can help you to think about how to structure this type of conversation with your boss. A few hard conversations can reduce your financial independence timeline by years (or decades).

The worst you'll hear is a simple "no" or "sorry, that's not in the budget right now." But more often than not, your boss will start thinking about what it would cost to replace you, and how much of a headache that would be. That alone can make them more open to discussing a raise. You have more leverage than you think.

## Change Industries or Jobs

What if you could do the same exact job that you're doing right now, but make double the money? If you're currently working in a low-paying industry, this could be your reality. A marketing job at a tech company might pay twice as much as the same job at a nonprofit or a local paper.

The title might be the same, but the salary bands aren't. Same role, same workload, but a very different income. If you're going to put in the same effort, why not do it where the compensation ceiling is higher? Industries like tech, healthcare, energy, and finance tend to pay more than traditional media, nonprofits, and education.

If you're not sure which industries are worth exploring for your current role, you can explore sites like Glassdoor, Payscale, or Salary.com and search your job title—for example, "administrative assistant." You might be surprised by how much more you could be earning elsewhere.

Once you spot a few companies offering better compensation for the same role, find a few people who work there and reach out. You can message them on LinkedIn, send an email, or connect however you can. Ask about their job, what they like about the company, and anything else you're curious about.

The best career moves often start with casual conversations, not formal interviews. If you're not sure how to do this, consider these sample scripts you can try:

- "Hey [Name], I'm thinking of switching jobs and saw that you're working as a [Job Title] at [Company]. How do you like it? Any chance I could pick your brain for 5-10 minutes?"

- "Hi [Name], I'm thinking about a job change and came across your profile. Any insights you can share about working at [Company] as a [Job Title]? Happy to chat via message or hop on a quick call if that's easier!"

My friend Justin saw his salary jump by $60,000 *twice*. Once by changing industries, and a second time by changing jobs within the same company he was already working in. These massive pay bumps drastically reduced his timeline for financial freedom, which he was able to reach by age 30. The bottom line is that one of the fastest ways to increase your salary is to change industries or jobs. In fact, employees who change jobs typically earn 10–20% more than those who stay put.

## Become an Intrapreneur

We've all heard about entrepreneurship, but what about intrapreneurship? An intrapreneur is someone who acts like an entrepreneur—but *within* a company. They take initiative, solve problems creatively, and drive innovation, all while using the company's resources and support. Intrapreneurs think like owners, even though they don't own the business.

Most employees simply go through the motions, counting down the hours until their shift ends, and their bosses treat them accordingly. But when you take initiative and look for ways to improve your team or company, you'll start to stand out quickly.

Intrapreneurs do things like:

- Propose projects that drive revenue or cut costs.

- Document their impact in terms of dollars, time saved, or results improved.

- Ask for performance-based incentives like bonuses or partial ownership.

- Communicate like a peer, not just a worker. They show how their work moves the business forward.

This approach won't work in every company—but when it does, it can be a game-changer. Below are a few sample scripts that might apply to your current role. Use what fits, adapt what doesn't, and leave the rest.

- "I've noticed we've had a few onboarding delays recently. I'd love to take the lead on creating a more efficient process for new hires. I think it could really streamline the first 30 days and free up time for the team."

- "I've been thinking about how we could improve the client onboarding process. Would it be helpful if I drafted a proposal or led a small pilot project to test a few changes?"

- "There's a lot of data we've been sitting on in [system/tool]. If you're open to it, I'd love to take on a small analytics project to see if we can pull out some actionable insights."

- "I've had some ideas for improving our workflow between departments. Would you be open to letting me run a quick experiment or mockup process to see if it could reduce handoff times?"

- "I've been reading about [relevant method/tool] and think it might be a great fit for how we do things. Would it be okay if I explored that and reported back with suggestions?"

The more you can lighten your manager's workload or help them succeed, the more leverage you'll gain when it comes to time off, raises, and getting the projects you want.

## Skill Building for The Future

Even if you can't picture yourself working in corporate forever, your job can still be a launchpad—not just for money, but for future opportunities. Use your role to:

- Learn and master new tools (CRM software, analytics platforms, A.I.)

- Improve communication skills (clear emails, concise updates, better questions)

- Mentor junior staff or train new hires to strengthen your leadership skills

- Build a personal portfolio of results (projects, metrics, wins you can point to)

- Strengthen your strategic thinking—learn how to spot opportunities, solve problems, and contribute beyond your job description.

One of the coolest parts about building skills as a working adult is that you can get *paid* to learn. Remember spending 12+ years in school without earning a dime? Now, you're in a position where your job can actually fund your education.

You can attend conferences on the company's dime, take free classes or certifications, or volunteer for new projects and stretch assignments—all during work hours. This is intrapreneurship in action: taking initiative inside your company to grow your skills, boost your value, and help the business at the same time.

The more skills, certifications, and experiences you stack while working, the more valuable you become—not just in your current role, but across the entire job market. As my friend and mentor Grant Sabatier says, "Skills are future currency." Jobs can disappear, industries can change overnight, and technologies can disrupt entire careers, but the skills you've built stay with you.

## CASE STUDY: JUSTIN TAYLOR

*Financial freedom age: 30*

Justin Taylor is a testament to what's possible when you focus entirely on maximizing your day job. Growing up in rural Mississippi, raised by a single mother who came from extreme poverty, he learned to be resourceful, self-sufficient, and disciplined with money. Those values followed him into adulthood. After earning a Computer Engineering degree—paid for through scholarships, financial aid, and Air Force ROTC—he graduated debt-free with a small cushion of savings. His first job after college paid $45,000 a year.

In 2015, at age 25, Justin discovered financial independence and began tracking every dollar. That awareness shifted how he approached his career. Instead of waiting passively for raises, he became intentional about increasing his value and positioning himself for higher-paying roles. Over the next several years, he made two strategic career moves—one internal shift and one leap to a new industry. Each career change increased his salary by about $60,000. His income grew from $4,500 per month in 2015 to more than $21,000 per month by 2022, entirely from his day job.

As his earnings rose, Justin kept his expenses remarkably low. His monthly spending typically ranged between $1,200 and $3,500, depending on where he lived, and even after reaching FI, he spent only around $2,300 a month. Every raise widened the gap between his income and expenses—fueling aggressive investing. His net worth grew from $38,000 at age 25 to more than $2.7 million less than a decade later.

Justin credits his success to systems, intentionality, and asking better questions. He automated everything, gamified his savings goals, and approached decisions through first principles. He reverse-engineered his ideal life—travel, growth, meaningful relationships—and shaped his career around that vision.

Today, Justin is fully retired and travels the world with his wife, Leslie, crafting a life centered on purpose and self-discovery. He hasn't felt a moment of boredom. "Once you remove the excuse of money," he says, "you're left with who you really are. And that's where the real work (and fun) begins."

Fun fact: Justin is also the co-host of my podcast, The Financial Independence Show!

## Call to Action: Make Your Job Work for You

If any part of this chapter resonates with you, pick one thing from this chapter and put it into motion this week:

- Ask your manager what success looks like for your role

- Set up a meeting to revisit your compensation

- Research salary bands for your job at better-paying companies

- Suggest a new project or initiative to implement

Your day job doesn't have to be forever—but while you have it, make it work as hard as possible for you.

# CHAPTER 9

# NETWORKING

*"You can have everything in life you want if you will just help enough other people get what they want."*

— ZIG ZIGLAR

Financial independence might start with math—but it accelerates with people. One unexpected connection can completely change your life (it's happened to me more than once).

Networking has led me to:

- Land an $80,000/year job right out of college

- Organize a 3-month book tour across the U.S.

- Build a multi–7-figure digital products business

- Get a free Tesla for a two-week vacation in Hawaii

Your network—friends, coworkers, mentors, business partners, and even online connections—can radically shift your financial path. The right introduction, insight, or opportunity can shave years off your journey to FI.

You don't need to be the most extroverted person in the room. You just need to be intentional. In this chapter, we'll break down how to build real relationships, grow your income, and unlock doors that might otherwise stay closed.

## Putting in the Reps

Networking is a skill—just like basketball, writing, or playing the piano. The more reps you put in, the better you get.

During my freshman year of college, I joined the Investing Club. I figured I'd learn how to pick winning stocks and get rich. But what I got was something far more valuable.

At our very first meeting, one of the seniors gave us a surprising homework assignment: reach out to three new people on LinkedIn *every single day*. It didn't matter if it was an alum, someone at a company we were curious about, or just someone with an interesting job. The goal was simple. Send three messages a day.

I won't lie—clicking "send" that first time was scary. But really, what did I have to lose? The worst that could happen was… nothing. And most of the time, that's exactly what happened. What I didn't realize at the time was that I was building one of the most valuable skills you can have: networking.

Most of those messages went unanswered, but a few turned into job opportunities, event invites, mentorships, and even lifelong friendships. Looking back, this one habit, and the relationships it sparked, played a massive role in how I was able to reach financial independence by age 25.

The actions you'll take from this chapter might just be the most important in the whole book.

## Networking the "Right" Way

The best networkers don't start with "What can you do for me?"—they start with "How can I help?" Offering value without expecting anything in return has been one of the most effective strategies in my entire networking journey.

I never lead with an ask. Instead, I look for ways to be helpful—whether that's sharing someone's content, connecting them with a useful contact, or sending a thoughtful message. No pressure. No agenda. Just real value.

One of my favorite examples of this happened in 2018 when I met Grant Sabatier from MillennialMoney.com. We were both at a conference called FinCon, and on the last day, I saw him standing near the door, so I took my shot. I walked over, introduced myself, and a simple hello turned into a two-hour conversation.

He had just finished writing his book, *Financial Freedom*, and was telling me about the enormous amount of work that went into it and how it was coming out in a few months. Expecting nothing in return, I asked, "How can I help?" and that one question led to a three-month road trip across the U.S., spanning 16,000 miles and more than 90 events.

Now, you don't need to go plan a national book tour, but you *can* find meaningful ways to support the people you want to connect with. Make it worth their time. Be genuinely curious. Be helpful first.

If you're struggling to connect with the "big names," try reaching out to people a few steps ahead of you instead. You might not hear back from a CEO, but someone just a few years further down the path is often more willing (and able) to help.

When I was job hunting, I reached out to people just a bit older than me who were working in interesting roles. I'd ask about their experience and how they liked their job. One of those cold messages turned into a real friendship, then a referral, and eventually, an $80,000/year job offer.

And last, try to connect with the person on a human level. Nobody wants to be cold-pitched by a robot. If you learn that the person you're reaching out to loves skiing, and you do too, talk about skiing. If they're a Harry Potter fan and so are you, talk about Harry Potter.

Networking doesn't have to feel forced. Find some common ground and start there. You can always get to the more business-focused conversations after you've established a real connection.

## Finding Opportunities and Mentors

One of the best places to start networking is within your existing circle. That next big opportunity—a job offer, a side hustle lead, or a valuable connection—might already be sitting in your contact list or following you on social media. Even if you don't know someone directly, chances are one of your friends, relatives, or neighbors does. A warm introduction from someone you trust can open doors you didn't even know existed.

Thinking about starting a side hustle? Ask around. See if someone within your network has already tried it. Want to switch industries? Browse your connections on LinkedIn or Facebook to see who's already working in that space. These people are far more likely to respond (and more willing to help) because there's already a connection in place.

Gold City Ventures, my digital products business, began with a simple message to another personal finance podcaster, Julie Berninger. I reached out to her and said, "Hey, I love the work you're doing. We should start some kind of business together. Any ideas?" That simple message eventually grew into a multi-seven-figure company.

Most of us already have a phone full of contacts and a social feed full of people we haven't talked to in years. Scroll through your texts, DMs, or LinkedIn connections. Who's doing something interesting? Who could use a word of encouragement or a quick check-in? The best connections often come from people already in your orbit.

Again, even if you're reaching out to a total stranger, find common ground to make your message more relatable. Maybe they went to the same school, support the same sports team, or share a hobby. Mention it! A message like, "Hey, I saw you work at [Company]—how do you like it? I'm thinking about applying. Also, I saw you went to Coastal Carolina—my friend went there too!" is far more likely to get a response than something cold or generic.

Networking isn't supposed to be robotic or transactional. Be genuine. Be interesting. Be someone they'd actually want to talk to.

The same approach works for finding mentors. Even if you're not job hunting or starting something new, connecting with someone a few steps ahead of you can provide insights, guidance, and opportunities you'd never access on your own. A good mentor can help you grow faster, avoid costly mistakes, and navigate your journey with more confidence.

As Jim Rohn famously said, "You are the average of the five people you spend the most time with." But in the age of the internet, "spend time" doesn't have to mean in person—or even in direct conversation. During my own FI journey, I "spent time" with dozens of mentors through podcasts, YouTube videos, blogs, and audiobooks. Most of them have no idea they were mentors to me, but their stories and lessons shaped my thinking and showed me what was possible.

Sometimes you just need to see someone else do something before it becomes a possibility for you. In 1954, Roger

Bannister became the first person to run a sub-four-minute mile. Within a decade, more than 300 athletes had done the same. They didn't know Bannister personally, but his example expanded the limits of what they believed they could achieve.

Before reading this book, you might never have heard of anyone retiring before 30, but now you've seen real case studies, strategies, and tactics from people who've done exactly that. Even if you never speak to any of them directly, simply knowing it's possible might be the unlock you need to push forward.

With all that being said, choose your mentors wisely. A mentor should be someone who's already in a position you'd like to be in—not just someone who happens to offer advice. Don't fall into the trap of listening to well-meaning friends or family members who haven't walked the path you're trying to take. My life would look very different if I had taken the "advice" of some of the people around me when I was getting ready to leave my job.

Be careful who you listen to, and intentional about who you learn from.

## Keep Track of Your Connections

Networking isn't just about meeting people. It's about staying in touch. Back when I was still in college, doing my 3 reachouts per day, I created a spreadsheet to track every person I talked to. I logged their name, contact info, title, where I met them, and one interesting detail they shared so I could follow up in a personal way. I still use a version of that today.

Columns include:

- Name

- Email or contact info

- What they do

- Where we met

- Last time we connected

- Notes or shared interests (e.g., "went to UMass," "loves mountain biking," "has a 7-year-old son who plays baseball")

Here's a sample:

| Name | Email | Title | First Met | Connected | Notes |
|---|---|---|---|---|---|
| John Smith | johnsmith12@ gmail.com | Personal finance podcaster | FinCon 2023 in New Orleans | 07/25/2025 | Going to Hawaii in October, big surfer |
| Jane Brown | janebrown83@ yahoo.com | Successful Etsy seller (JaneSells) | Reached out to her via Instagram in August 2025 | 10/13/2025 | Loves hiking, spends winters in Puerto Rico |
| Willy Tops | willytops47@ gmail.com | Multi-family real estate investor | Local real estate meetup in 2024 | 06/02/2025 | Runs marathons, lives in Philly |

My networking sheet has over a thousand rows at this point. Once a month, I scan the sheet and reach out to a few people

I haven't talked to in a while. A short message goes a long way, and it keeps relationships alive that could lead to something meaningful down the line.

It might not be the right time now, but you might reach out to someone for the 7th time, and they say, "You know what, a position just opened up at my job that I think you'd be perfect for", or "I'm actually just starting X business, looking for someone to help me scale it!"

I sound like a broken record at this point, but you just *never* know what opportunities lie on the other side of a message.

## Sample Scripts: Reaching Out

Reaching out can feel awkward. I remember how cringy I felt sending out my first couple of messages on LinkedIn. These low-pressure scripts are easy ways to start a conversation or reconnect.

### To a new contact on LinkedIn/Facebook/etc.:

> *"Hey [Name], saw that you're a [job title] at [Company Name]. I've been doing some research, and it looks like a great fit for me. How are you liking it?"*

### To someone you haven't talked to in a while:

> *"Hey [Name], I saw your post about [topic]—really cool stuff! Would love to catch up sometime soon if you're up for it. It's been too long!"*

**To someone you just met or briefly interacted with:**

*"Hey [Name], great meeting you at [event/group]! I really enjoyed our conversation about [topic] and would love to stay in touch."*

I always try to include something small and personal in each message I send. You don't want your outreach to feel like a copy-and-paste job. Taking just a few seconds to personalize your message shows the other person that you've done your homework, and that you're genuinely interested in connecting, not just blasting out a mass message.

As your relationship grows, keep track of the little details in your notes (I use that same spreadsheet for this). It might seem small, but remembering something like their daughter's dance recital from six months ago can seriously impress. You don't need an amazing memory, just a system that helps you show up thoughtfully.

## Like-Minded Communities

Networking doesn't always have to lead to a job, client, or business opportunity. Sometimes, the most valuable thing you can gain from networking is community—people who share your goals, ask great questions, cheer you on, and make the journey less lonely.

I had read dozens of books, listened to hundreds of podcasts, and watched countless videos about financial freedom. But it wasn't until I attended an event called CampFI in 2018 that everything started to feel *real*. I met a couple who retired at 29 and 30. I met another guy who retired at 28. I talked with multimillionaires who looked and acted just like regular people. That weekend completely shifted my perspective. Financial freedom suddenly felt achievable. It lit a fire under me, and reminded me just how powerful it is to be surrounded by people who *get it*.

If you're looking to connect with people on a similar path, go where they already are. That could mean:

- Local personal finance meetups (ChooseFI groups, Mustachians, Bogleheads)

- Business or entrepreneurship networking events

- Online communities (Reddit, Discord, Facebook, LinkedIn)

- Conferences like CampFI, FinCon, or EconoMe

Not sure where to start? Try Googling: "[Your City] + personal finance meetup" or join a few Facebook groups related to financial independence, entrepreneurship, or freelancing.

I've now traveled the world, built businesses, and shared some of my best memories with people who were at one point just random strangers on the internet or at an event.

## CASE STUDY: GRANT SABATIER

*Financial freedom age: 30*

Grant Sabatier's journey to financial independence began from a moment of urgency. After graduating with a philosophy degree and no student loans, he still found himself carrying over $20,000 in credit card debt. His first job paid $47,000, but within a few years, he was unemployed, back at his parents' house, and staring at a bank balance of just $2.26. Money had always been a source of stress growing up, and now it demanded his full attention.

Everything shifted the night he typed "how to make money" into Google. That single search led him to the FIRE movement and put him on an entirely new path. He made a bold decision: he would reach financial independence in just five years. Grant dove headfirst into learning digital marketing, teaching himself through free resources, online communities, and by connecting with people who could help him improve faster. As his skills grew, he began proactively reaching out to potential clients—lawyers, schools, recruiters, and more—to land freelance work. What started as small gigs quickly snowballed into a thriving consultancy, and eventually a digital agency earning over $300,000 per year.

Even as his income surged, Grant kept his expenses grounded. He lived simply, rented modest apartments, drove inexpensive cars, and avoided anything that didn't contribute to his long-term vision. Most of his earnings went directly into investments, especially low-cost index funds like VTSAX, along with cash reserves to fuel business opportunities. His net worth climbed rapidly, and he hit his goal ahead of schedule—achieving full financial freedom at age 30, just six years after starting his journey with $2.26 in the bank.

Today, Grant's life is built around freedom, family, and pursuing projects that genuinely interest him. He follows his curiosity, embraces creativity, and makes decisions based on impact, not necessity. "I get to do what I want, when I want, with who I want," he says. "That's the real wealth."

Grant's story is a powerful example of how quickly life can change when you stay curious, take action, and surround yourself with the right people. Networking, learning, and reaching out for help didn't just accelerate his career, they helped unlock the path to a completely different future.

## Call to Action: Reach Out

Break the ice and reach out to at least one person. This could be someone interesting in your contact list, or a completely new connection. It's up to you. Offer encouragement. Ask a question. Share something helpful. Your next opportunity might be one message away.

Want to grab the exact networking spreadsheet I've used for 10+ years? Grab your copy at retireby30book.com/resources.

# SECTION 4

# INVESTING

# CHAPTER 10

# WHY INVEST?

*"Compound interest is the eighth wonder of the world.
He who understands it, earns it; he who doesn't, pays it."*

— ALBERT EINSTEIN

Most people either think investing is complicated, gambling, or a combination of the two. Roth IRAs, 401(k)s, compound interest, high-yield bonds, growth stocks, reverse mortgages, HELOCs—it all sounds so confusing. And that's exactly what the financial industry wants. But the truth is, investing can be easy and automated.

This chapter will show you why investing isn't optional if you want to build wealth, and how even small amounts, consistently invested, can completely change your future.

## Why You Can't Save Your Way to Wealth

Saving is essential, but saving alone isn't enough. Let's walk through a simple case study comparing a saver (Jimmy) and an investor (Donna).

Both Jimmy and Donna start at age 25. They work decent jobs, manage their expenses, and have $500 left over at the end of each month. Jimmy puts his $500 into a traditional savings account earning 0.5% interest. Donna, on the other hand, invests her $500 in the stock market, earning an average return of 8% per year.

Fast forward 40 years to age 65, and the difference between the two is staggering.

|  | Monthly Contribution | Return Rate | Years | Total Invested | Total (with interest) |
|---|---|---|---|---|---|
| Jimmy | $500 | 0.5% | 40 | $240,000 | $264,953 |
| Donna | $500 | 8% | 40 | $240,000 | $1,554,339 |

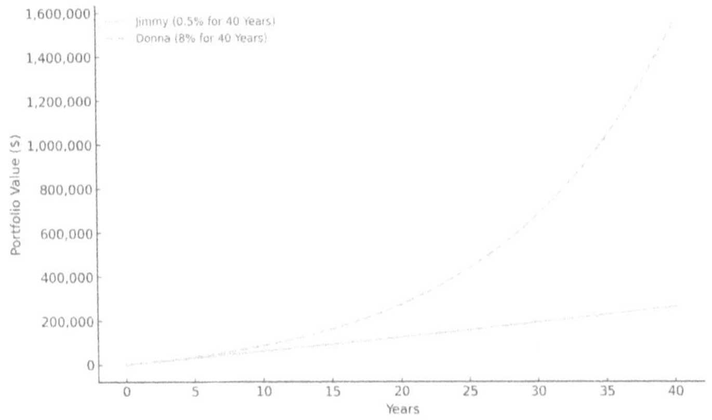

After 40 years, Donna has almost $1.3 million in additional wealth, just from choosing to invest instead of save. If you want to run some numbers yourself, type in "compound interest calculator" into Google and prepare to have your mind blown. Saving instead of investing can cost you millions in the long run, as you saw in the chart above, and so can waiting. Let's make up two more people and have some fun mathing.

Lucas and Arielle both learn about financial freedom and start investing $500 per month. The only difference is that Lucas is 25 years old and Arielle is 35 years old. They contribute their $500 per month religiously until age 65.

|  | **Monthly Contribution** | **Return Rate** | **Years** | **Total Invested** | **Total (including interest)** |
|---|---|---|---|---|---|
| Lucas | $500 | 8% | 40 | $240,000 | $1,554,339 |
| Arielle | $500 | 8% | 30 | $180,000 | $679,699 |

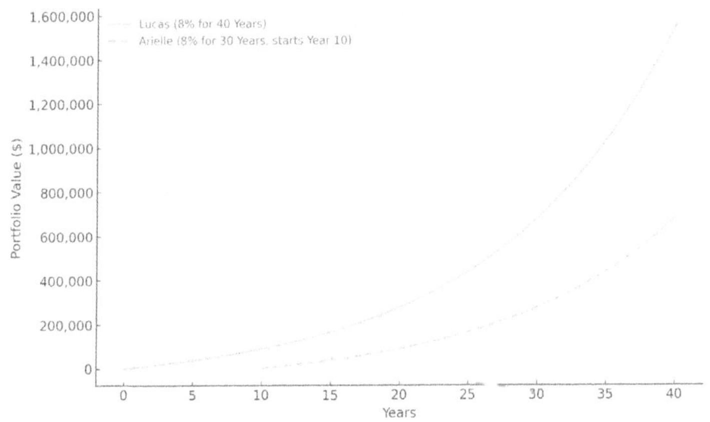

With just a 10-year head start, Lucas ends up with over $850,000 more than Arielle by age 65, despite only contributing $60,000 more in total. Remember, he was investing $500 a month—or $6,000 a year—for an extra 10 years. That's the power of starting early.

Whether it's $5 or $500 a month, the key is to start investing now. It's easy to put it off until your next promotion, after you buy a house, or once the holidays are over, but forming the habit now is what your future self will thank you for.

And if you are thirty-five and already feeling behind in all this, don't. Better to start today than to have never started at all. While it may be too late to gain the benefits of compound interest like you could at twenty-five, you can absolutely benefit more from starting now than if you waited until you are forty-five. Time is more powerful than how much you invest, or even what you invest in. It's the single most important variable you control, especially when you're young.

To really drive this home, let's add a third person to the mix: Larry. After hearing about Lucas and Arielle, Larry decides to turn his financial life around at age 50. He earns significantly more than both of them, but he has far less time to invest. Determined to catch up, Larry commits to investing $2,000 per month for the next 15 years, until he reaches 65.

| | Monthly Contribution | Return Rate | Years | Total Invested | Total (including interest) |
|---|---|---|---|---|---|
| Lucas | $500 | 8% | 40 | $240,000 | $1,554,339 |
| Arielle | $500 | 8% | 30 | $180,000 | $679,699 |
| Larry | $2,000 | 8% | 15 | $300,000 | $651,650 |

Even though Larry was contributing *quadruple* the amount that Arielle was, he was only investing for half the time, and, come retirement age, he actually has less money than her. Have I convinced you to start investing yet?

The sooner you begin—even with small amounts—the more freedom you create for your future.

## The Doubling Penny

Would you rather have $1,000,000 or a magic penny that doubles every day? When surveyed, most people instinctively pick the $1,000,000, but this is wrong.

At first, the penny doesn't seem like much. After 5 days, it's only 16 cents. But by day 20, it's over $5,000. And by day 30, that penny has grown into more than $5 million. That's the power of compound growth. It starts slow, then suddenly takes off—and the longer it has to grow, the more dramatic the results.

Now, your wealth isn't going to double every day (and if it does, call me), but the more often your money doubles, the wealthier you'll become. You've probably heard the saying "the rich get richer," and it's true, because once someone builds meaningful wealth, each doubling leads to massive gains. Turning $50 into $100 isn't life-changing. Even $500 into $1,000 doesn't move the needle much. But $500,000 into $1,000,000? Or $5,000,000 into $10,000,000? The bigger the numbers get, the more exciting each doubling becomes.

If you need a little motivation to start investing early, try using the Rule of 72. It's a simple, back-of-the-napkin way to estimate how long it will take your money to double. Just take 72 and divide it by your expected annual rate of return. For example, if you expect an 8% return, your money will double roughly every 9 years (72 ÷ 8 = 9).

$$\text{The Rule of 72} = \frac{72}{\text{Rate of Return (\%)}}$$

- At 8% returns, it doubles every 9 years (72 / 8)

- At 10%, every 7 years (72 / 10)

- At 12%, every 6 years (72 / 6)

Let's put the Rule of 72 into action. Say you invest $100,000 at age 25 and earn an average annual return of 8%. Based on the rule, your money should double roughly every 9 years.

By age 34, you'll have $200,000.
By 43, $400,000.
By 52, $800,000.
By 61, $1.6 million.
And by 70, $3.2 million.

Mind you, this is without ever contributing another dollar. All of this growth is just from that original $100,000 invested at age 25. That's the magic of compound interest.

## What Happens If You Don't Invest?

Let me be blunt: if you don't invest, your only options for retirement are Social Security, a pension (if you're lucky), or a pile of cash earning basically nothing.

According to the 2023 Federal Reserve Survey of Consumer Finances, the median retirement savings for Americans aged 65-74 is just $200,000. That's not enough to retire for most people. Even if you're saving diligently, inflation slowly eats away at your money's purchasing power. Investing is how you outpace inflation, grow your money, and create real financial options.

A dollar saved today won't be worth a dollar tomorrow. At 3% inflation, what costs $100 today will cost over $200 in 24 years. That's why you can't afford to let your money sit idle.

## What If You're Scared to Lose Money?

Everyone is. No one wants to watch their hard-earned dollars drop 20% in a market downturn. It's normal to feel anxious about market drops—but the long-term data tells a different story:

- Over any 1-year period, the market has historically been positive about 75% of the time.

- Over any 10-year period, it's positive about 94% of the time.

- Over 20 years, it's never lost money.

The real risk isn't losing money in the market. It's missing out on decades of growth because you never got started.

Investing feels scary until you realize the biggest threat to your future wealth is actually doing nothing at all. Start small, stay in the game, and let time do what it's always done—turn patience into profit.

In the next three chapters, we'll cover the three main types of investments I've used to build wealth and achieve financial freedom: the stock market, real estate, and alternative investments.

## Call to Action: Run the Numbers

Search "compound interest calculator" online and start playing around with the numbers. Try entering different monthly contributions and time horizons. You might be surprised by how quickly things can grow.

Tip: I like to use an 8% average annual return to stay on the conservative side (even though the stock market has historically averaged around 10% over the past few decades). Feel free to adjust that number up or down as you see fit.

In the next chapter, we'll break down exactly how the stock market works, and how to start investing with confidence, even if you're brand new.

# CHAPTER 11

# THE STOCK MARKET

*"The stock market is designed to transfer money from the active to the patient."*

— WARREN BUFFETT

The stock market can feel intimidating—charts, jargon, ticker symbols, and headlines designed to stir panic or hype. But at its core, the stock market is just a tool. A tool that, when used wisely, can help you build wealth, generate passive income, and accelerate your path to financial independence.

You don't need to be a Wall Street analyst to invest successfully. You also don't need to pay a financial advisor to manage your investments. You just need a basic understanding of how the system works, and a simple, repeatable strategy to stick with over time.

Let's break it down.

## What the Stock Market Has Done Over Time

The stock market isn't a get-rich-quick machine. It's a wealth-building engine. But it works best over long stretches of time. If you're expecting your money to double overnight (like the magic penny we discussed in the last chapter), you're out of luck. Wealth building rewards the patient.

Over the past 100 years, the stock market has averaged ~10% per year before inflation. Some years were brutal (like 2008: -37%). Others were euphoric (like 2013: +32%). But if you zoom out, the trend is clear: long-term investors win.

This chart shows the stock market's trajectory over the past century. Even through wars, recessions, crashes, and pandemics, the market has continued climbing. Not because it's magic, but because companies continue to grow, innovate, and generate profits.

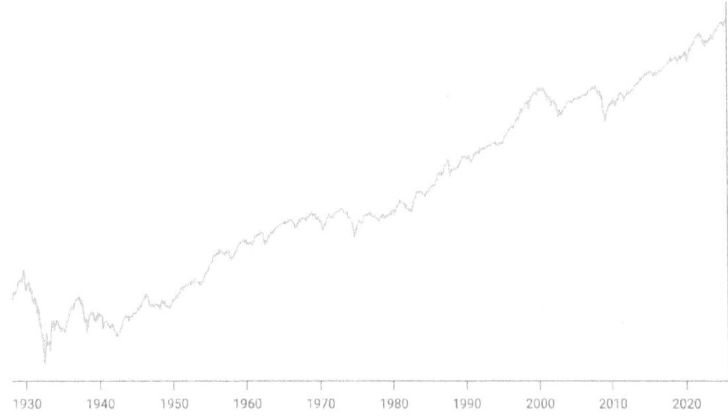

At its core, the U.S. stock market represents thousands of companies across the country. When the overall economy grows, the stock market tends to go up. When the economy shrinks, the market generally declines. In a growing population, a capitalistic system, and a world constantly expanding into new industries and innovations, it's no surprise the stock market has continued to rise over time.

Brian Feroldi, author of *Why Does The Stock Market Go Up*, said it best "The stock market goes up because companies solve problems. "That's the point of a business: to solve others' problems. Since problems will always exist, companies will continue growing. They generate profits, reinvest, grow, and pass value to shareholders.

Sure, the stock market is volatile in the short term, but over the long run, it trends up and to the right. That's why patience and a long-term mindset are key.

## How the Stock Market Works

When you buy a stock, you're buying a tiny piece of ownership in a company. If that company earns more profit over time, reinvests, and grows, your share becomes more valuable. It's as simple as that. (We'll get into how to buy stocks later in this chapter, but it's important to understand how they work first.)

Imagine your friend opens a new restaurant. To get it off the ground, they need money, so they decide to split the business into 100 equal shares and sell some of those shares to investors.

You buy 10 shares for $100 each, investing a total of $1,000. Now, you own 10% of the restaurant.

As the restaurant grows—more customers, higher profits, maybe even another location—your shares become more valuable. If the business is now worth twice as much, your shares might be worth $200 each. You could sell them for a gain, or hold onto them and keep earning a portion of the profits.

Now imagine that instead of one restaurant, you could invest in thousands of different businesses. That's essentially what investing in the stock market allows you to do. You're buying ownership in real companies—like Apple, Starbucks, and Home Depot—and as they grow and earn more money, so do you.

## Investing Isn't Just Picking Stocks

Now, all this talk about stocks might make it sound like I'm a stock picker, constantly hunting for the next big company to make a fortune. But that couldn't be further from the truth.

Stock picking *sounds* exciting. You imagine finding the next Apple or Tesla and watching your money grow 10x overnight. But the fact is: most people (and even most professional fund managers) can't consistently beat the market. Picking individual stocks takes a ton of time, research, and luck. Even then, you're probably not going to win long-term.

That's why I stick with index funds, which I'll discuss shortly. They're simple, low-cost, and give you instant diversification across hundreds or thousands of companies. Instead of trying to guess which company will crush it next, I'd rather own a small piece of everything and ride the average.

When I first started investing, I was *all-in* on stock picking. Sometimes I won, sometimes I lost. I'd spend hours every day researching companies, listening to earnings calls, and trying to find some kind of "edge" to beat the market. I kept this up for years. The result? I actually underperformed the market by a little, and wasted hundreds of hours I'll never get back. The stress wasn't worth it either. I was constantly checking my stock picks, freaking out over every headline. I became obsessed with my portfolio.

When I finally stopped trying to beat the market and automated my investments into index funds, everything got easier, and more profitable. I've never looked back.

## Plants and Gardens

If a stock is a plant, then an investment account is the garden where the plant can grow. Weird analogy, I know—but stick with me.

Investment accounts—like 401(k)s, IRAs, and brokerage accounts—are the gardens. Inside those accounts, you choose your *investments*, like index funds, stocks, or bonds—the plants.

You might use an IRA, a 401(k), or a regular brokerage account as your garden. Each garden has different rules for taxes and access. But it's the plant inside—your actual investment—that determines how your wealth grows.

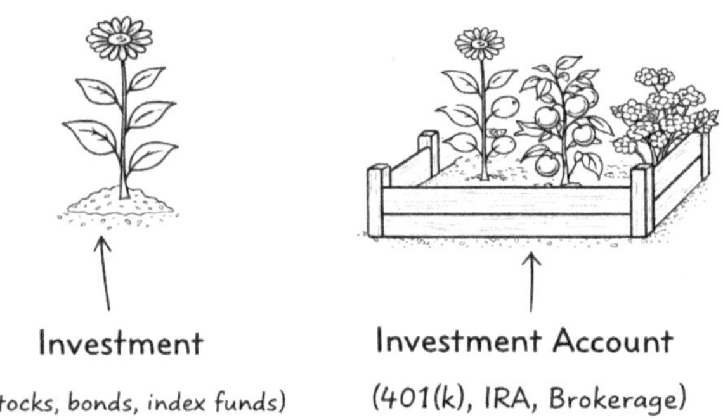



Before we start talking investment strategy, let's quickly define some of the main account types (the gardens):

- **Traditional 401(k):** Offered through your employer. Contributions are made pre-tax, which lowers your taxable income today. Many employers offer a match (e.g., 100% of the first 5%). That's free money, so don't leave it on the table.

- **Roth 401(k):** Also offered through your employer, but contributions are made with after-tax dollars. You don't get a tax break today, but your money grows tax-free, and you won't owe any taxes on withdrawals in retirement (as long as you follow the rules). Employer matches are typically made on a pre-tax basis, even if your contributions are Roth—though some plans now allow Roth employer matches as well.

- **Roth IRA:** Funded with after-tax dollars. Your money grows tax-free, and qualified withdrawals in retirement are also tax-free. It's a great option for younger investors or anyone who expects to be in an equal or higher tax bracket in retirement, since you pay taxes when you put the money in. Roth IRAs have income limits.

- **Traditional IRA:** Funded with pre-tax or after-tax dollars, depending on your situation. Contributions may be tax-deductible based on your income and access to an employer plan. This is a great option for anyone who expects to be in a lower tax bracket in retirement, since you pay income taxes when you take the money out.

- **Brokerage Account:** This is fully taxable, with no contribution limits or withdrawal restrictions. It s ideal for flexibility, early retirement goals, and accessing funds before age 59½ without penalties.

- **HSA (Health Savings Account):** Triple tax advantaged—contributions are pre-tax, growth is tax-free, and withdrawals are tax-free *if used for qualified medical expenses*. After age 65, you can withdraw for any reason—non-medical withdrawals are taxed as ordinary income, similar to a Traditional IRA. It requires enrollment in a high-deductible health plan (HDHP), but it is one of the most tax-efficient accounts available.

Within each garden, you have investments, or your "plants". Here are some terms that will be helpful to know as we move through the rest of this chapter:

- **Stock**: A stock is a small piece of ownership in a company. When you buy a stock, you're buying a share of that company's future growth and profits.

- **Bond**: A bond is basically a loan you give to a company or the government. In return, they agree to pay you interest over time and give you your money back later.

- **Mutual Fund:** A mutual fund is a type of investment where your money is pooled with other investors to buy a mix of stocks, bonds, or other assets. Sometimes, it's actively managed by a fund manager who tries to beat the market by picking what they think are the "best" investments. That active management usually comes with higher fees.

- **Index Fund:** An index fund is a specific *type* of mutual fund that's passively managed. Instead of trying to beat the market, it simply aims to match the performance of a market index—like the S&P 500. Since no one's hand-picking stocks, index funds typically have much lower fees.

- **ETF:** An ETF is pretty similar to a mutual fund. It's a bundle of investments that gives you broad exposure to the market, but it trades like a stock. That means you can buy and sell ETFs throughout the day at market prices. Think of it like a mutual fund with a bit more flexibility.

If this feels overwhelming, don't worry—you don't need to get everything 100% perfect to build wealth. Some investment strategies are more optimal than others, but simply getting started already puts you ahead of the average person. We'll walk through the investing process step by step later in this chapter.

And I know I've thrown around terms like "tax-advantaged," "after-tax," and "pre-tax"; don't stress if they're unfamiliar. We'll break them down with clear examples in the chapter on tax optimization.

## The Order of Operations

When you're first starting, it's easy to overthink. *Where do I put my next dollar? How do I prioritize?*

Here's a simplified investing flow that I recommend to friends and family:

1.  **Build a small emergency fund ($1–3K).** You don't want to invest yourself to $0. Keep a small cash cushion in case of emergency.

2.  **Get your 401(k) match.** A 100% match on the first 5% you contribute to your 401(k)? That's an instant 100% return. Get that free money.

3.  **Pay off high-interest debt.** This is especially true of anything above 7–8%. If you're unsure, compare your interest rate to the long-term historical return of the stock market (around 10% before inflation).

4.  **Max out your IRA.** Whether you choose a Roth or a Traditional IRA depends on your specific situation

(more on this later), but maxing out your IRA each year gives you tax benefits you don't want to miss.

5. **Max out your 401(k) or equivalent.** If your employer offers a tax-advantaged account like a 401(k), 403(b), or 457(b), make sure you use it. These funds aren't always "locked away until retirement" the way many financial gurus claim (more on this later).

6. **Max out your HSA (if available).** It's one of the most tax-efficient investment accounts available, though contribution limits are relatively low, and non-medical withdrawals before age 65 are subject to taxes and penalties. An HSA is only available to those with a high-deductible health plan.

7. **Taxable brokerage account.** No tax perks—but no withdrawal restrictions either. Great for early retirees or general wealth building.

You don't need to follow this formula to a tee. Everyone's situation is unique. You may not have access to some of the accounts listed here, and you might have access to others that aren't included. This is simply a guide to remove the guesswork and help you invest with confidence.

Again, we're still talking about the investment accounts (gardens) here. These are what will hold your investments (plants). We'll get to choosing the right investments for you in the next section.

## Investment Considerations

Financial jargon is designed to be confusing, but once you understand a few key terms, you'll be able to make informed, confident decisions about where and how to invest your money.

### *Expense Ratios*

Expense ratios are one of the sneaky ways that people get taken advantage of by financial advisors and institutions. An expense ratio is the annual fee an investment firm charges to manage your mutual fund or ETF.

As of this writing, the industry average is 1.01%, which may not sound like much, but just wait until we math it out. Many index funds at brokerages like Vanguard, Fidelity, and Schwab charge as little as 0.03%. Let's walk through another scenario to see just how big a difference this actually makes.

Iris and Max both invest $500 per month for 40 years, earning an average annual return of 8%. Iris invests in an actively managed mutual fund and pays a 1.01% fee. Max sticks with low-cost index funds from Vanguard, paying just 0.03% in fees. Historically, low-cost index funds outperform most actively managed funds, but for the sake of this example, let's assume both funds earn the same 8% return before fees.

Over 40 years, here's the difference between the two investors:

- Iris pays 1.01% in fees and ends up with $1,308,727.
- Max pays just 0.03% in fees and ends up with $1,730,420.

Difference: $421,693

That's nearly half a million dollars lost to fees, just from a 0.98% difference. This is why low-cost index funds matter so much. Tiny percentages don't feel like a big deal today, but over decades, they quietly eat away at your future wealth.

Expense ratios are public info, and you can usually find them with a quick Google search or on the fund's website. Always check before you invest. Low fees = more money in your pocket.

*Risk Tolerance*

Investing is about more than just numbers on a screen. Emotions play a huge role, and a major loss can lead to stress, anxiety, or even full-blown panic. That's why it's so important to understand your risk tolerance—how much volatility you can realistically handle without freaking out or abandoning your plan.

One of the best ways to manage that risk is by choosing the right mix of stocks and bonds. Now, you might be thinking, *"Didn't Cody say he doesn't like picking individual stocks or bonds?"* You're absolutely right.

When I talk about stocks and bonds in the next few examples, I'm not referring to individual companies like Tesla, Amazon, or Nike. I'm talking about the entire stock market and the entire bond market. You can invest in both through broad, diversified index funds—like a Total Stock Market Index Fund or a Total Bond Market Index Fund. These are the exact types of funds I invest in myself.

Stocks are more volatile in the short term. They can swing up and down wildly. But over the long term, as we discussed in the last chapter, they've historically gone up—a lot. Bonds, on the other hand, are much more stable. They don't grow nearly as fast, but they tend to be more stable and often hold up better during stock market downturns. They inch upward slowly and steadily, like a financial tortoise.

Now, it might sound like I'm trashing bonds here, but that's not the case. Bonds absolutely have a role in your portfolio. As JL Collins, author of *The Simple Path to Wealth*, puts it: "Bonds help to smooth the ride." When stocks are down 30% one year and up 35% the next, bonds help keep things a bit more stable. They don't offer huge returns, but they tend to hold steady, and that can help you sleep better at night.

If you're not comfortable watching your portfolio drop 30% or more during a market crash, then yes, adding bonds might be a smart move.

Let's walk through a simple example. We'll look at three investors who each start with $100,000 but have different risk tolerances, and therefore different mixes of stocks and bonds. All three plan to stay invested for the next 30 years. Now let's see how a freak event, like a 50% stock market drop, would affect each of their portfolios. Using historical averages, we'll assume:

- Each investor starts with $100,000.

- Stocks earn an average annual return of 10.1%.

- Bonds earn an average annual return of 5.5%.

- And during the hypothetical 50% crash in this example, bond values remain stable.

Let me introduce you to Daring Doug, Mild Mindy, and Worried Winston.

**Daring Doug's Portfolio**: 100% Stocks.

- Portfolio value immediately after the market crash: $50,000

- Portfolio value 30 years later: $896,581

**Mild Mindy's Portfolio**: 50% Stocks. 50% Bonds.

- Portfolio value immediately after the market crash: $75,000

- Portfolio value 30 years later: $697,488

**Worried Winston's Portfolio**: 100% Bonds.

- Portfolio value immediately after the market crash: $100,000

- Portfolio value 30 years later: $498,395

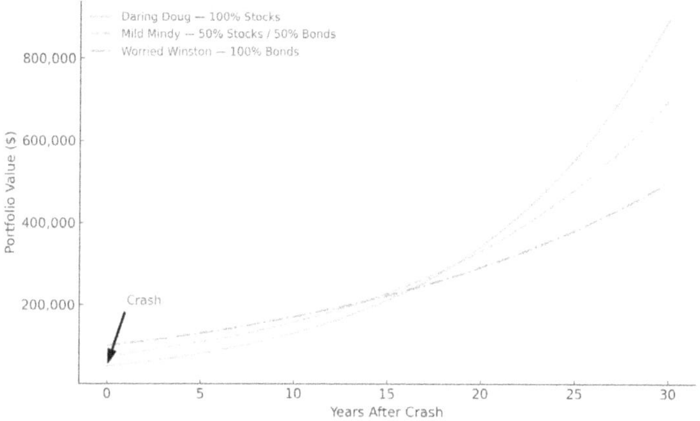


As you can see, Worried Winston's portfolio was unaffected by the market crash, but 30 years later, his portfolio is worth $398,186 less than Daring Doug's portfolio. Mild Mindy is right in the middle. She didn't suffer too much of a loss during the market crash and earned a modest return over the next 30 years.

Yes, Daring Doug ended up with the highest returns over the 30 years from that original $100,000 investment, but that doesn't mean a 100% stock portfolio is always the right move. Depending on your goals, timeline, and how much risk you're comfortable with, it might make sense to include some bonds in your portfolio, even if they offer lower returns. Let's consider which might be the best fit for you by looking next at your investment horizon.

*Investment Horizon*

As we covered in the risk tolerance section, stocks can be volatile. They go up and down. And while they've historically gone way up over the long term, what happens if you need that money in 6 months, 2 years, or even 5 years?

That's where the investment horizon comes in—understanding *when* you'll need each dollar you're investing. One of the most common reasons I hear for not investing is "I have a big expense coming up," like a home purchase, wedding, or car. But that doesn't mean you shouldn't invest. It just means you need to be more strategic about it.

Let's say you're planning to use $50,000 for a house down payment next year (which, by the way, is probably more than you need—but we'll get into that in the next chapter). The last thing you want is to have all that money in stocks, the market drops 30%, and now you're forced to sell your investment while it's down.

Instead, set aside what you *know* you'll need for that big purchase in a lower-risk investment, like a Total Bond Market Index Fund. Then, put anything extra into long-term investments like stocks. If your goal is early retirement, I'd recommend keeping only the bare minimum in low-volatility investments—just enough to cover near-term costs. The rest should be working hard for you in higher-growth assets. You don't want to end up like Worried Winston from earlier— playing it too safe and missing out on massive growth. Most of your money should be given the chance to compound and accelerate your wealth.

If I had kept everything in bonds—or worse, in a checking account (gasp!)—I'd have millions less today. Understanding your investment horizon is one of the most important tools for building wealth *and* sleeping well at night.

## Diversification

Diversification is reducing risk by spreading out your investments. In other words, diversification means you aren't putting all of your eggs in one basket.

The best part about index funds and ETFs is that they have built-in diversification. Since these securities are an aggregation of thousands of other stocks or bonds, they are inherently diverse. Let's see how diversification affects an investor. This example will also show you why I prefer index funds over individual stocks.

Derek and Janine both have $100,000 to invest. Derek loves technology, so he invests his entire $100,000 in an up-and-coming tech stock. Janine, on the other hand, decides that she wants her investments to be more diversified. She invests her $100,000 into a Total Stock Market Index Fund, which includes thousands of companies, and also a small piece of that same up-and-coming tech stock.

The following day, the company that Derek invested in declares bankruptcy, and he loses his entire $100,000 investment. Janine's portfolio value drops from $100,000 to $99,980.

How is this possible? Well, Derek invested in an up-and-coming stock, which gave him partial ownership in the company in the form of shares. When the company went bankrupt, the value of Derek's shares went to $0. Janine invested in the Total Stock Market Index Fund. The up-and-coming tech stock only made up 0.02% of the index fund, so when the company declared bankruptcy, Janine's investment value decreased by only $20.

Imagine the U.S. stock market as one large block made up of thousands of smaller squares. Each square represents a company, and the size of the square reflects how big that company is relative to the rest of the market.

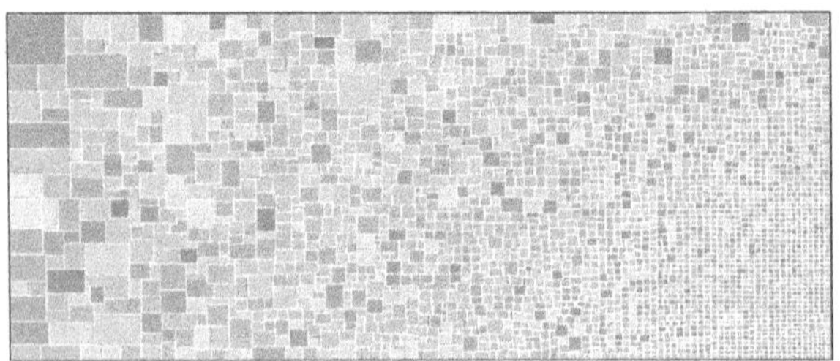


That's why I always recommend investing in index funds and ETFs. They offer built-in diversification. Instead of trying to pick the next big winner, you can simply invest in the total stock market and still earn historically strong returns, around 10.1% per year.

## How to Start Investing (Step-by-Step)

Now that you have a bit of understanding about the stock market and investing, let's get to the fun part: How to actually start investing. I'm going to break it down step by step, so that you'll know exactly how to set up your account(s) and your investments.

Let's dive in.

### Step 1 - Pick a Low-Cost Brokerage

A "brokerage" is just a fancy financial term for a company where you can invest your money. "Low-cost" means that they offer investment options with minimal fees. Vanguard, Schwab, and Fidelity are all solid options. Simply go to one of their websites and start the sign-up process.

### Step 2 - Choose Your Account Type

Start with an IRA, or open a taxable brokerage account. This is where your actual investments reside. Remember the garden analogy from earlier? The IRA or brokerage account is your "garden," and your investments are the "plants" that grow inside.

You need the garden (investment account) set up first, so you have somewhere to put your plants (your investments).

### Step 3 - Link Your Bank Account

To invest, you need money in your account. Once you've entered your personal details during the signup process, link your bank account to your new investment account.

### Step 4 - Start Investing

If your goal is to retire as quickly as possible, you'll likely want to keep most of your portfolio in stocks (through index funds, of course). During my own financial independence journey, over 90% of my portfolio was in total stock market index funds like VTSAX (Vanguard), SWTSX (Schwab), or FXAIX (Fidelity).

If any of these funds have minimum investment requirements you can't meet yet, you can always start with their ETF equivalents—like VTI (Vanguard).

*Step 5 - Automate & Chill*

Once your account is set up and you've made your first purchase, schedule recurring investments—whether weekly, biweekly, or monthly. That way, your money grows automatically without you having to think about it.

The goal is simple: buy and hold for the long term. Don't panic when the market dips. Investing doesn't need to be complicated. Start small, stay consistent, and let time do the heavy lifting.

## Building Your Portfolio

If you become stressed about what to invest in—whether you'll lose money, how much to contribute, or how often the market goes up and down—come back and re-read this chapter. Let this be your constant reminder of the long-term security and benefits of investing. If you're a numbers person, look at the stats we covered and the graph we reviewed that showed the bounce back after a 50-percent market crash thirty years later.

Every early retiree's portfolio looks a little different. There isn't just one path to financial freedom. That's why it's called *personal* finance. One person might go all-in on stocks, while another adds bonds because they'll need some of that money soon for a house. Your investment mix should fit your goals, timeline, and comfort level.

And don't feel like you need to copy my "total stock market index fund only" strategy. If you prefer to include international funds, great. Want to dabble in a few individual stocks? Go for it. Don't want to max out your 401(k)? That's fine. The key is understanding the basics. Even if your strategy isn't perfect, being 90% of the way there is enough to build serious wealth.

And if the stock market isn't your thing, that's okay too. Maybe you want to buy real estate, acquire a small business, or take a different approach with your money. In the next chapters, we'll look at other investment strategies you can use to reach financial independence and retire early.

## CASE STUDY: PURPLE

*Financial freedom age: 30*

Purple built her entire path to financial independence on one simple strategy: consistently investing in the stock market. Raised by a single mother who taught her to avoid debt and live within her means, she grew up frugal by necessity. But it wasn't until she entered adulthood—graduating debt-free with a Communications degree and earning $35,000 a year—that she began channeling that frugality into investing. As she job-hopped and negotiated her way into higher salaries, she sent nearly every extra dollar straight into VTSAX, the Vanguard Total Stock Market Index Fund. No real estate. No bonds. No complicated strategies. Just steady, automated investing in broad-market index funds.

Her FI journey began in earnest in 2015, when she finally embraced the FIRE movement her partner had introduced years earlier. Once she ran the numbers, she set a ten-year plan to retire by 35. But thanks to a simple investing approach and a widening gap between income and expenses, she ended up beating that target by five years. She'd already been tracking her finances for years, growing her net worth from $5,000 in 2011 to over $53,000 by 2014. As her salary climbed above $100,000, her expenses dropped to as low as $17,000 per year. Every dollar she saved went directly into the stock market.

Her net worth growth reflected both her discipline and the strong bull market during her accumulation years. By 2015, she had $89,000 invested. In 2017, she crossed $234,000. In 2019, she reached $448,000. And in 2020, at just 30 years old, she retired with $620,767—100% invested in VTSAX, supported by a modest cash buffer for flexibility.

Perhaps the most powerful part of her story is what happened next. Even without meaningful earned income in retirement, her portfolio kept growing. The same simple stock-market strategy that got her to FI helped her wealth compound into a seven-figure portfolio. She crossed $1 million in net worth several years after leaving her job—clear evidence of what long-term investing, low costs, and patience can do.

Today, Purple is a full-time nomad, living out the freedom she built through disciplined saving and stock-market investing. She spends her days traveling, writing, running, birdwatching, practicing yoga, enjoying good food and sunshine, and nurturing deep relationships. Her life after FI is joyful, intentional, and deeply aligned with her values, all made possible by a straightforward, stock-market-only investment strategy.

Note: "Purple" isn't her real name, but her story is as real as any. She chose the pseudonym for her blog, A Purple Life, so she could share her finances openly while maintaining her privacy.

## Call to Action: Start Investing

If you're not already investing, there's no better time to start than today. Open an account and put in your first dollar. It takes just 15–20 minutes.

If you're already investing, use this chapter as a chance to review your strategy. Is there room for improvement? Are there account types you're not using yet? Are you confident in the portfolio you've built?

Do this now, before moving on to the next chapter. Seriously. It's way too easy to keep putting it off and then end up wishing you had started 10 years ago.

# CHAPTER 12

# REAL ESTATE

*"Don't wait to buy real estate. Buy real estate and wait."*

— WILL ROGERS

Real estate is one of the most powerful and tangible wealth-building tools out there. It's not perfect. It's not 100% passive. But for many people on the path to financial independence, real estate has been the single biggest lever.

You can use it to create cash flow, hedge against inflation, build equity, and even live for free. Plus, there are more ways to invest in real estate today than ever before.

## Why Real Estate is So Powerful

Real estate offers something the stock market doesn't: control.

You can negotiate deals, raise rents, reduce expenses, and force appreciation through renovations. You can borrow money at fixed interest rates and let tenants pay off the loan. And you can generate cash flow every month, not just long-term gains.

But it's not just the control, it's the flexibility. Real estate allows you to scale slowly or rapidly. You can self-manage or outsource. You can reinvest the profits or refinance to pull equity out tax-free. It's one of the few investments where you can directly influence the outcome.

It also offers unique tax advantages: depreciation, 1031 exchanges, mortgage interest write-offs, and more. These can significantly boost your returns in ways the average investor never sees with stocks. (You'll learn more about this in the tax optimization chapter.) Plus, it's often more intuitive. The fact that real estate is a physical, tangible asset brings some investors more comfort than the abstract nature of stock-market investing.

Real estate is also one of the best hedges against inflation. While your fixed-rate mortgage stays the same for 30 years, rents often rise with the cost of living, meaning your profit margins improve over time. Even in economic downturns, rents tend to be sticky. They might drop slightly, but people always need a place to live.

Before this chapter starts sounding like an ad for buying real estate, let me be clear: real estate is not passive. Unlike the stock market, it requires a lot of upfront effort. You'll need to manage repairs, deal with tenants, and keep track of moving parts.

By the end of this chapter, you'll have a better sense of whether real estate investing is right for you—and if it is, which type of investing best fits your skills, goals, and interests.

## Types of Real Estate Investing

When most people think about "investing in real estate," they think about buying a home and renting it out. But there are so many different ways to make money with real estate. There's no one-size-fits-all approach. Here are some of the most common paths:

### House Hacking

Buy a property, live in one unit, and rent out the others. Or, if you're in a single-family home, rent out the extra rooms. This strategy—known as house hacking—is how I got started. It cut my housing costs to less than zero and allowed me to build equity while living for free.

Our first property was a three-family home in Connecticut that we bought for $235,000. On the main level were two side-by-side duplex-style units, each with three bedrooms and one bathroom. In the back, down in the basement, was a one-bedroom, one-bath apartment where Lauren and I lived. The two top units brought in $2,200 in combined rent each month, while our all-in expenses—including the mortgage, insurance, utilities, maintenance, and reserves—were only $1,700 per month. Instead of paying $2,000 in rent like many of our peers in the city, we were living for free and actually earning $500 a month from our housing.

As I mentioned before, house hacking comes in many different shapes and forms. If buying a multi-family property isn't an option, you can still house hack with a single-family home by renting out the extra bedrooms. My friend Jesse Ray did exactly that, and he was able to retire by 28.

One of the biggest advantages of house hacking is that, if you plan to live in the property, you can qualify for an owner-occupant loan with as little as 3.5% down. That low barrier to entry is why I recommend house hacking so often to new real estate investors.

### Long-Term Rentals

This is the classic strategy: buy a property, rent it out to tenants on year-long leases, and hold it for long-term cash flow and appreciation. The month-to-month income might not be as high as with short-term rentals, but the consistency and predictability are often much better.

After our first house hack, we bought our first long-term rental just a few months later—a duplex right down the road for $170,000. The two units brought in $2,250 per month in rent, while our all-in expenses were only $1,350. Unlike house hacking, though, if you're not living in the property, you'll typically need to put down at least 20% of the purchase price. For a $500,000 property, that means an $80,000 down payment, plus closing costs, legal fees, and other expenses.

Fortunately, since my income had been increasing from my digital products business, Gold City Ventures, I had enough money coming in to afford the 20%+ down payments for these long-term rental properties.

That first year, we went all in and bought a total of 11 rental units. That decision was a huge factor in reaching financial independence by age 25. At first, we were flying blind and had no clue what we were doing. But as we built better systems, managing those 11 units only took 4–5 hours of our time each month.

And that's the key: systems. Most of the people who complain about being landlords either have poor systems or no systems at all. Learn how to screen tenants, manage payments, handle repairs, and maintain the property. With the right systems in place, long-term rentals can be a reliable and scalable path to wealth. We'll cover specific property management strategies later in this chapter.

### Short-Term Rentals

Short-term rentals have exploded in popularity, and for good reason. The income potential is often far higher than traditional long-term rentals. I've had Airbnbs earn three to five times more each month than a comparable long-term unit.

Our first short-term rental was a three-bedroom, one-bath home in Massachusetts with lake access. As you can imagine, it was a huge hit in the summer. We listed it in May, and by August, it had its first $10,000+ month. If we had rented it out long-term, we probably would've made around $2,000 a month instead.

Of course, not every month brought in five figures, but even after accounting for slower seasons, that property averaged over $6,000 per month in the first year, or about three times what we would've made as a long-term rental.

That said, short-term rentals come with more work and moving parts. You'll need to furnish the property, handle bookings and turnovers, and stay compliant with local regulations. But when done right, with solid systems, a reliable cleaning crew, automation tools, and smart pricing, they can generate serious income and accelerate your path to financial freedom.

### REITs

REITs (Real Estate Investment Trusts) are one of the easiest, most hands-off ways to invest in real estate. When you buy into a REIT, you're investing in a company that owns or finances income-producing properties like apartment complexes, shopping centers, or industrial buildings.

Using the plant-and-garden analogy from earlier, a REIT is another type of "plant." You can invest in REITs inside your IRA, brokerage account, or 401(k), just like you would an index fund. The trade-off is that you don't get the same tax advantages, equity buildup, or level of control that come with owning property directly. Still, REITs are a great way to diversify your portfolio or get exposure to real estate without having to buy and manage a property yourself.

### Crowdfunding

Real estate crowdfunding lets you invest in real estate projects without buying an entire property yourself. Instead, you pool your money with other investors to fund large-scale deals like apartment complexes, commercial buildings, or vacation rentals. It's a middle ground between REITs and direct ownership. It has more control and higher potential returns than a REIT, but is still relatively passive. You don't have to deal with tenants, maintenance, or financing headaches; just invest and let someone else handle the details.

Many of my real estate investments today are in a specific type of crowdfunding called syndications. Syndications are essentially group investments where multiple investors pool their money to buy a large property—something that would be difficult or impossible to purchase individually—like an apartment complex or self-storage facility. In most syndications, there's a sponsor (also called the general partner) who finds the deal, manages the property, and handles all the day-to-day operations. Then there are limited partners—the passive investors who contribute capital and share in the profits.

I've found most of my syndication deals through networking, but there are also plenty of reputable crowdfunding platforms you can invest through such as FundRise, RealtyMogul, and CrowdStreet. Just keep in mind that these investments are typically illiquid, meaning your money will be tied up for several years. It's also important to thoroughly vet both the sponsor and the deal before investing.

For investors looking for hands-off exposure to real estate with strong potential returns, crowdfunding can be an excellent option.

*Flips*

This is the HGTV model: find a fixer-upper, renovate it, and sell it for a profit. When done right, flipping can generate huge lump sums of cash in a short amount of time But it's definitely a high-risk, high-reward strategy.

I've seen plenty of people get burned by flipping because they assumed an "if I build it, they will come" mindset. Unfortunately, that's rarely how it works. Success in flipping comes down to doing your homework—researching the market, running the numbers, finding reliable contractors, and having a clear exit plan. Done right, it can be incredibly profitable. Done wrong, it can be a nightmare.

On my latest flip, we went $45,000 over our projected renovation budget. Thankfully, we had some cushion built in and still turned a profit, but I'd be lying if I said it wasn't stressful. If the market turns or you uncover a major issue with the property, you could easily end up stuck holding the bag.

Now, before I completely scare you off, flipping *can* work. I made $118,000 in profit from my first flip. But not all of them go that smoothly, and I've heard more than enough horror stories from new investors who jumped in too fast. If you want to experiment with flipping, start by finding a general contractor you trust. Research each property thoroughly before making an offer. Estimate the purchase price, repair costs, and expected sale price, and then bump your repair budget by 50%. If the numbers still work, and you're comfortable with a bit of risk, go for it.

## *Wholesaling*

Wholesaling involves finding off-market properties, getting them under contract at a discount, and then assigning that contract to another buyer for a fee. You never actually buy the property, you're simply the middleman who connects the seller and the buyer.

This strategy can be lucrative if you're skilled at networking, marketing, and negotiation. I know investors who've made anywhere from $5,000 to $100,000 per deal without ever owning the property. But it takes time, hustle, and a lot of repetition to get good at it.

With wholesaling, speed is everything. You need to sell the contracts quickly, which usually means having an established buyer list or a strong network of real estate investors. If you're the kind of person who can sell ice to an Eskimo, this could be a real estate strategy worth exploring.

## Real Estate Strategy Comparison Chart

We've explored a lot of real estate options. To quickly reference the many options and what they entail, you can study the chart below.

| Strategy | Capital Needed | Time Required | Risk Level | Cash Flow Potential | Scala-bility | Passive or Active |
|---|---|---|---|---|---|---|
| House Hacking | Low | Moderate | Low-Moderate | Moderate | Moderate | Active |
| Long-Term Rentals | Moderate | Low-Moderate | Moderate | Moderate | High | Semi-Passive |
| Short-Term Rentals | High | High | High | High | Moderate | Active |
| REITs | Very Low | Very Low | Moderate | Moderate | High | Passive |
| Crowd-funding | Moderate | Very Low | Moderate - High | Moderate | Moderate | Passive |
| Flips | High | Very High | High | High (Lump Sum) | Low | Active |
| Whole-saling | Very Low | High | Moderate | Low-Moderate | Moderate | Active |

There are dozens of real estate strategies out there, and I'm not going to claim there's one "best" way to reach financial independence. Beyond the ones we've already covered, there's also self-storage, commercial real estate, mobile homes, glamping, land flipping, boutique hotels—and plenty more.

On my own path to financial freedom, I started with house hacking and long-term rentals, while the short-term rentals, flips, and syndications came later. Since my first ventures into real estate focused on buying and holding rental properties (rather than REITs, crowdfunding, or wholesaling), I want to share some of the lessons I learned along the way, so you can learn from my experience and accelerate your path to FI.

## What to Know Before You Buy

Before you start scrolling Zillow or touring open houses, it's worth slowing down and learning the basics of the home-buying process. Whether you're buying a house hack, long-term rental, or short-term rental, a little preparation goes a long way, and can save you thousands in the process.

When we bought our first property, we thought we had done our research. We'd run the numbers, crunched our budget, and talked to a lender. But once we actually started the process, we realized how much we *didn't* know—things like how much to save for closing costs, how important the inspection and appraisal really are, and how to find the right agent.

Here are some of the biggest lessons we learned along the way:

**1. Know your financing options.** Not all loans are created equal. FHA loans allow you to put as little as 3.5% down, while VA loans (for eligible veterans) offer 0% down options. Conventional loans typically require 5–20% down but come with fewer restrictions. Shop around with multiple lenders to compare interest rates, fees, and loan types. You might be surprised at how much you can save over the life of the loan.

**2. Find the right market.** When I first started searching for deals, I was priced out of my local market near Boston. Everything felt too expensive, and the price-to-rent ratios just didn't make sense. But when I expanded my search and started to explore different cities and states, suddenly, the math worked. I could buy multifamily properties at a fraction of the cost, and the cash flow was significantly stronger. You don't need to buy in your backyard. Look for cities with affordable housing, strong rental demand, and price-to-rent ratios that make sense. And when you find one deal that works, you can often repeat the formula in the same area.

**3. Budget for more than just the down payment.** Most first-time buyers forget about closing costs, which can run 2–5% of the purchase price. You'll also need to cover things like inspections, appraisal fees, and prepaid expenses such as property taxes and homeowners' insurance, plus any immediate repairs. As a rule of thumb, try to have *at least* an extra 5% of the purchase price saved beyond your down payment, because unexpected costs always show up.

**4. Get a good agent (and know what they do).** A good real estate agent can make the entire buying process much easier. They'll help you understand market values, negotiate with the seller, and handle all the paperwork. Don't just go with your friend's cousin who "does real estate on the side." Interview multiple agents and choose someone who knows your local market and understands your goals, especially if you plan to house hack or invest. A good agent can also act as your quarterback, leading and organizing your real estate team, including your lender, attorney, and contractors.

**5. Don't skip the inspection and appraisal.** These two steps protect you. The inspection identifies potential issues (like foundation cracks, roof problems, or mold) before you're locked in. The appraisal confirms that the home's value matches the price you're paying—something your lender cares a lot about. Don't cut corners here.

**6. Keep your emotions in check.** It's easy to fall in love with a house and overpay. Remember: this is both a home *and* an investment. Stick to your numbers and be willing to walk away if a deal doesn't make financial sense. There will always be another property.

**7. Plan for after closing.** Once you get the keys, the work doesn't stop. Set aside a repair fund, change the locks, set up utilities, and review your property taxes and insurance. If you're house hacking, start lining up tenants early so you're not scrambling once you move in.

As *Rich Dad Poor Dad* author Robert Kiyosaki famously said, "You make your money when you buy." In other words, your profit is often determined the day you purchase the property, so take your time and do thorough due diligence before buying your first one.

## Managing Rental Properties

Buying rental properties is just the first step. The real key to success—and to keeping your sanity—is how you manage them. Property management doesn't have to be a full-time job. With the right systems in place, it can be surprisingly hands-off.

When people say managing rentals is "hard," it's usually because they don't have proper systems or a reliable team—or both. The landlords who struggle the most are often the ones collecting rent in cash, doing every repair themselves, or skipping proper tenant screening.

If you put in the work upfront—building systems, setting clear processes, and finding good help—rental management doesn't have to take much time at all. We now manage our 13-unit portfolio in just four or five hours per month. Here's what made the difference:

**1. Screen tenants carefully.** Your tenants are your business partners—treat them that way. Run credit and background checks, verify income, and always call references. I also like to trust my gut after meeting them in person. A good tenant makes your life easy; a bad one makes it miserable.

**2. Set clear expectations upfront.** Have a strong lease that spells out rent due dates, late fees, maintenance responsibilities, and rules for the property. Go over the lease with new tenants so there are no surprises later. The fewer assumptions, the fewer headaches.

**3. Automate everything you can.** Use property management software like *Avail, Buildium,* or *Apartments.com* to collect rent automatically, handle maintenance requests, and store documents. The less manual work you have to do, the more scalable your portfolio becomes.

**4. Build your "A-Team."** Keep a list of trusted professionals— plumbers, electricians, handymen, HVAC techs—who you can call when something breaks. Having reliable people on speed dial turns emergencies into minor inconveniences.

**5. Decide if (and when) to hire a property manager.** If you hate dealing with tenants or live far from your rentals, a property manager might be worth the 8–10% fee. They'll handle leasing, repairs, and rent collection so you can focus on finding your next deal.

**6. Keep good records.** Track every expense, receipt, and repair. Not only does this make tax time easier, but it also helps you spot trends and plan for long-term maintenance.

The key to managing rentals efficiently is systems. Every process—from screening tenants to fixing leaks—should be repeatable. Once those systems are in place, rental properties can truly become "passive income."

## The Power (and Risk) of Leverage

Consider this: when buying real estate, you can control a $400,000 asset by putting just $14,000 down (3.5%) with an FHA loan or certain low-down-payment conventional loans. Imagine being able to buy $400,000 worth of stocks for $14,000. It sounds incredible, right? But it's a double-edged sword. That same $14,000 down payment also means you're carrying a $386,000 loan, and that kind of leverage comes with risk.

Let's look at a separate example of leverage in action.

Assumptions:

- Home price: $500,000
- Annual home appreciation: 1%

- Monthly rental income per property: $5,000

- Monthly mortgage on leveraged properties: $2,000

- Monthly non-mortgage expenses (taxes, maintenance, etc.): $1,500

Now that we've got our numbers, both Investor A and Investor B have $500,000 to invest.

Investor A decides to buy five separate rental properties using 20% down on each. With each property costing $500,000, she puts down $100,000 per property (we'll ignore closing costs for simplicity).

Investor B, on the other hand, doesn't like debt. He uses all $500,000 to buy one property outright in cash.

Here's what that looks like each month:

Investor A's five properties bring in $25,000 in total rent, minus $10,000 for mortgages (*$2,000* × *5*) and $7,500 for other expenses (*$1,500* × *5*), leaving $7,500 in monthly cash flow. Investor B's one property brings in $5,000 in rent, minus $1,500 in expenses, for $3,500 in monthly cash flow.

Now let's look at appreciation. After 10 years, each $500,000 property is worth about $552,311. Investor A's five properties gain a total of $261,555 in equity (*$52,311* × *5*). Investor B's single property gains $52,311 in equity. As time goes on and rents rise, leverage magnifies these returns even more. But remember, that same leverage works both ways.

Let's flip the scenario. Imagine the housing market crashes right after both investors buy. Property values and rents drop by 25%. Each home is now worth $375,000, and rent falls to $3,750 per month. Investor A now owns five houses worth less than their $400,000 mortgages—she's underwater. Her cash flow drops from $7,500 to just $1,250 per month (*$18,750 rent – $10,000 mortgage – $7,500 expenses*). Investor B's single property is also worth less, but since he owns it outright, he still earns $2,250 per month (*$3,750 rent – $1,500 expenses*). If both investors can't find tenants, Investor A still owes $10,000 a month in mortgage payments—no matter what. Not ideal.

Leverage is powerful when prices and rents are rising, but it can be brutal when the market turns. During the 2008 housing crash, too much leverage was a major reason many investors lost everything. Used wisely, leverage can accelerate your path to financial independence. Used carelessly, it can destroy it. Leverage amplifies everything—the good and the bad.

## Real Estate and Cash Flow FI

Real estate really shines when it comes to cash flow. If you're relying solely on stocks to fund your retirement, you'll need to wait until your portfolio hits 25 times your annual expenses— that's the 4% rule. So, if your goal is to live on $60,000 a year, you'd need a $1.5 million portfolio before you could safely withdraw 4% (or $60,000) each year.

With real estate, though, you can "cash flow" your way to financial independence much faster. The reason, as we discussed earlier, is leverage. Let's use the same assumptions as before:

- Home price: $500,000

- Monthly rental income per property: $5,000

- Monthly mortgage (on leveraged properties): $2,000

- Monthly non-mortgage expenses (taxes, maintenance, insurance, etc.): $1,500

Now let's bring back Investor A—the one who bought five properties—and introduce Investor C. Both have $500,000 to invest, and both need $60,000 per year in passive income to reach financial freedom.

Investor A buys five rental properties using 20% down on each. With each property costing $500,000, she puts down $100,000 per property (we'll ignore closing costs for simplicity). Investor C, on the other hand, goes fully passive and invests his entire $500,000 in a total stock market index fund.

Investor A's five properties generate $25,000 in rent each month. After paying $10,000 in mortgages (*$2,000 × 5*) and $7,500 in other expenses (*$1,500 × 5*), she's left with $7,500 in monthly cash flow. Since she only needs $5,000 per month to cover her expenses, she's officially financially independent—thanks to strategic leverage.

Using the 4% rule, Investor C can only safely withdraw $20,000 per year (*$1,667 per month*) from his $500,000 stock portfolio. He's only   of the way to FI. To reach $60,000 per year in safe withdrawals, he'd need roughly $1,500,000 invested in the stock market.

Again, leverage is a double-edged sword—but this example shows just how powerful it can be when used wisely. Some of the fastest financial independence stories I've seen have been through real estate.

In my own journey, I reached financial freedom with around $200,000 in down payments across four rental properties. Between 2020 and 2021, I bought:

- A 3-unit for $235,000

- A 2-unit for $170,000

- A mixed-use property for $315,000

- And another 3-unit for $245,000

Total rents came to $10,750 per month, with all-in expenses of about $7,050, leaving me with an average monthly cash flow of $3,700. At the time, my personal expenses were only around $2,000 per month, which meant my real estate cash flow alone made me financially independent.

I also had about $500,000 invested in the stock market, which provided a nice cushion—but at a 4% withdrawal rate, that only generated about $20,000 per year. Real estate and digital products are what truly accelerated my timeline and allowed me to reach financial independence in just three years.

Now, I'm not saying you *have* to invest in real estate. Plenty of people retire in under a decade using just index funds—or even more alternative strategies (which we'll cover in the next chapter). But if you're looking to reach financial independence as fast as humanly possible, real estate can be a powerful tool to help you get there.

## CASE STUDY: JABBAR ADESADA

*Financial freedom age: 21*

Real estate changed everything for Jabbar Adesada. By 21, he had built a portfolio worth more than $2.2 million and reached financial independence, despite starting with almost nothing. Jabbar grew up in an abusive household where money represented fear and control. He had no financial guidance, only a desire to escape the instability he was raised in. When he joined the military as his first job, taking home about $1,200 a month, he began saving aggressively, living on just $300 a month (made possible by the military), and teaching himself about personal finance through observation and curiosity.

He discovered financial independence in 2019 and began building momentum through small wins: investing in the stock market, picking up side hustles, and saving $30,000 in 2020 alone. But he quickly realized that if he wanted to accelerate his journey, real estate was the lever with the most potential. In 2021, he made the bold decision to liquidate his stock portfolio and purchase two properties valued at nearly

$1 million combined. One was a house hack that boosted his income immediately; the other—a short-term rental—brought in more than $4,000 a month.

Those first two properties changed the trajectory of his life. His income jumped from a few thousand dollars a month to more than $7,000, and the momentum didn't stop. By 2022, Jabbar had scaled to 10 rental units and built a real estate portfolio valued at over $2.2 million. The passive income from those properties reached $12,000 per month—enough for complete financial independence while barely into his twenties.

Throughout the journey, Jabbar kept his personal expenses extraordinarily low. He drove an old Prius, ate at the chow hall, skipped vacations, and funneled every dollar into investments and property. He didn't wait for perfect circumstances or complete certainty. Instead, he took calculated risks, learned quickly, and made decisions with urgency. "People waste too much time planning instead of doing," he said. His ability to act decisively allowed him to scale faster than others.

Today, Jabbar spends much of his time abroad and pours his time into building impactful businesses, traveling, and intentionally designing his ideal life. He describes financial independence as "a full reset"—a foundation that allows him to pursue big ideas and support others who come from backgrounds like his. Real estate didn't just help him reach FI quickly, it gave him a platform to reinvent his future.

## Call to Action: Start Researching

If any of the real estate strategies in this chapter resonated with you, take the next step and dig deeper. My goal was to show you the many different ways to invest in real estate, but it's up to you to decide which approach (if any) aligns best with your goals.

Run some numbers, get set up on the MLS, pick up a book on house hacking, or reach out to a real estate investor and ask questions. Real estate might be the key that helps you supercharge your journey to financial independence.

# CHAPTER 13

# ALTERNATIVE INVESTMENTS

*"If you want to have a better performance than the crowd, you must do things differently from the crowd."*

— SIR JOHN TEMPLETON

Not every dollar needs to go into index funds or real estate. Alternative investments are yet another way to reach financial independence, fast. But what exactly qualifies as an "alternative investment"? Generally, it's anything outside of traditional stocks, bonds, and real estate. These investments often carry more risk, less liquidity, and greater complexity, but also the potential for big upside if used wisely. Let's take a look at some of the most common types of alternative investments and how they might fit into your FI journey.

## Small Business

These are alternative investments that involve acquiring a small business—either online or in the physical world—to generate cash flow and long-term value. You're buying something that already works, rather than starting from scratch.

### Online Businesses

This includes buying digital assets like content sites, e-commerce stores, or SaaS tools. These can often be managed remotely, automated with systems, and scaled with digital marketing. Sites like Flippa or Empire Flippers showcase deals with existing revenue, traffic, and profit.

Chelsea Clark, a guest on one of my podcast episodes, shared how she started buying small websites with under-optimized content and simple monetization models. She wasn't a developer, just someone who learned how to grow and flip digital assets using SEO, affiliate programs, and clean content structures. By applying just a few improvements, she was often able to double or even triple a site's income in a few months, then either sell it for a significant profit or keep it as a cash-flowing asset.

Stories like Chelsea's show that investing in online businesses isn't about chasing unicorns. It's about spotting value, improving systems, and optimizing what already exists. You don't need to create the next Facebook; there are plenty of simple, "boring" online businesses that can generate the cash flow you need to reach financial independence.

If you have skills in SEO, copywriting, or paid ads, these businesses can become strong cash flow engines. But as with any investment, due diligence is crucial—watch out for fake traffic, high customer churn, or dependence on a single product or platform. Also, keep in mind that online businesses can be short-lived, so don't rely on them alone to fund your retirement for the next 50 years.

*Physical Businesses*

Sometimes the best way to start running a physical business is to buy one. Think laundromats, vending machine routes, car washes, or local service businesses like cleaning or landscaping. And you might be wondering, "Why would anyone sell a profitable business?" Simple: people retire, relocate, lose interest, or want to free up capital. Owners step away for all kinds of reasons, even when the business is doing well.

You can find these opportunities on platforms like BizBuySell, BizQuest, and BusinessForSale. Compared to online businesses, physical businesses usually require more capital, a local presence, and the ability to manage employees or vendors. But if you already have experience running a business—or you learn quickly—buying a small business can be a great way to "purchase" cash flow from day one.

I've seen people replace their W-2 income through a small business acquisition, but not without taking on some risk. My friend Brian Luebben, for example, bought a hood-vent cleaning company for $900,000 with just $60,000 down using creative financing. Like with real estate, you typically make a down payment and then finance the rest through seller financing, bank loans, or payment plans. You don't need to pay the full cost of the business upfront.

After just one month, Brian's hood-vent cleaning company was producing $4,000 a month in cash flow. Not bad. Brian has years of experience buying and improving businesses, and while this path doesn't make sense for everyone (it's far riskier and more hands-on than something like an index fund), it can be worth exploring if you have the right background. The key is buying the right business, optimizing operations, and then either managing it yourself or hiring someone you trust.

Now that we've talked about business-based alternatives, let's shift to a category that grabs headlines and sparks debates: speculative assets.

## Speculative Assets

This category includes investments with high volatility and high potential reward, so please invest wisely.

### Cryptocurrencies

Crypto is highly volatile, speculative, and definitely not for the faint of heart. Still, for a small portion of your portfolio, having some exposure to cryptocurrencies like Bitcoin or Ethereum might make sense, especially if you believe in the long-term potential of decentralized technology.

As of this writing, I keep about 3% of my net worth in Bitcoin and Ethereum. Since I started investing, I've seen wild price swings and unbelievable headlines. My general rule: I only invest in the established players, not meme coins or the latest up-and-coming token.

If you've made it this far in the book, I'm guessing your goal isn't to reach financial independence by winning the crypto lottery. For every story of a 20-year-old making millions on Dogecoin, thousands of others lost everything. Don't get caught up in the hype. If you do invest in crypto, stick with assets that have a more proven track record.

## Penny Stocks and Meme Stocks

Penny stocks are very low-priced shares (usually under $5) from small, often unproven companies, making them extremely risky and volatile. Meme stocks, on the other hand, are companies whose prices surge mainly because of online hype and social media momentum rather than business fundamentals. Both can be fun to dabble in, but they shouldn't make up a large part of your portfolio. These are the "lottery ticket" investments of the stock market: cheap, exciting, and fueled by hype and emotion more than fundamentals.

When I first started investing, I got caught up in that excitement. I'd throw money at penny stocks, hoping for a massive overnight return. Now and then, I'd catch a quick win, but more often than not, I'd end up losing money. The same goes for meme stocks. If you're constantly refreshing Reddit threads or watching stock charts like a hawk, you're probably not investing—you're speculating.

That said, it's okay to have a little fun with it. If you want to carve out 1–2% of your portfolio for speculative investments like penny stocks, meme stocks, or other high-risk plays, go for it. Just treat that money like entertainment, not a retirement plan. The bulk of your wealth should come from steady, proven investments—not the next viral stock on social media.

## Real Assets

This category includes physical, tangible assets that can hedge against inflation, offer long-term store-of-value potential, or generate modest passive income.

### *Gold and Commodities*

Gold and other commodities have been around as investments for centuries, and for good reason. They often hold their value when everything else feels shaky. When inflation rises or the stock market takes a hit, gold often acts as a hedge, helping stabilize your overall portfolio.

That said, while gold can provide some peace of mind, it shouldn't make up a large portion of your investments. Commodities don't produce cash flow like stocks or real estate, and over the long run, their returns have generally lagged behind other asset classes.

### *Farmland and Timberland*

Land and other resource-based investments offer slow but steady returns. They're tangible, often produce income through rent or harvested resources, and have historically acted as a hedge against inflation. Land, in particular, has long been viewed as a stable store of value—especially during uncertain times.

Platforms like AcreTrader have made land investing more accessible to everyday investors, but keep in mind that these are long-term, illiquid investments. You might have to wait several years before seeing returns, so this shouldn't be a large portion of your portfolio. A small allocation can add diversification and stability, but most of your wealth should still be in assets that grow and compound over time.

*Collectibles and Other Niche Plays*

Collectibles and other niche investments—like fine wine, art, vintage video games, or even Pokémon cards—are often driven by passion and scarcity. They can be fun to own and talk about, and in some cases, the upside can be huge. But they're also highly speculative and unpredictable.

If you enjoy collecting, there's nothing wrong with dedicating a small slice of your portfolio (or hobby budget) to these kinds of assets. Just don't invest money you can't afford to lose. Unlike stocks or real estate, collectibles don't generate cash flow, and their value depends entirely on what someone else is willing to pay. They can be a fun, personal way to diversify, but they shouldn't be your plan for financial independence.

## Lending and Private Equity

These alternatives generate returns by lending money or investing in private assets that often pay interest or dividends. They're usually riskier, but the returns can also be much higher.

Note: Some of these opportunities are only available to accredited investors—those with an annual income of at least $200,000 (or $300,000 with a spouse) for the last two years, or a net worth of $1 million or more (excluding your primary residence).

### Peer-to-Peer Lending

Peer-to-peer lending allows you to loan money directly to individuals or small businesses through platforms like Prosper or similar lending marketplaces. In exchange, you earn interest payments—essentially acting as the bank. The returns can be attractive, but they come with risk. If borrowers default or the economy slows down, your returns can disappear quickly.

### Hard Money Lending

Hard money lending involves loaning money to real estate investors or small businesses, usually secured by the property or asset itself. The returns can be attractive—often in the 8–12% range—but they come with higher risk. Successful hard money lending requires solid underwriting skills, a good understanding of the collateral, and a strong tolerance for uncertainty.

### Private Equity or Angel Investing

Private equity and angel investing involve putting money into early-stage startups or private businesses—often through crowdfunding platforms or investor networks like AngelList. The potential upside is massive, but so are the risks. Most startups fail, and your money can be tied up for years before you see any returns (if you ever do).

# How Do They Compare?

While alternative investments can play a role in your strategy, they typically carry more risk and less historical consistency than traditional assets like stocks and real estate. Here's how they compare:

| Investment Type | Liquidity | Historical Return | Cash Flow Potential | Risk Level |
|---|---|---|---|---|
| Index Funds | High | ~ 7—10% | Moderate | Low |
| Real Estate | Medium | ~ 8—12% | High | Medium |
| Online Business | Med-Low | ~ 10—30% | High | High |
| Physical Business | Low | ~ 15—30% | High | High |
| Cryptocurrencies | High | Highly variable | None | Very High |
| Penny / Meme Stocks | High | Highly variable | None | Very High |
| Gold/ Commodities | Medium | ~ 2—5% | None | Medium |
| Farmland/ Timberland | Low | ~ 5—8% | Moderate | Low-Med |
| Collectibles | Low | Highly variable | None | High |
| Peer-to-Peer Lending | Low-Med | ~ 4—8% | Moderate | Med-High |
| Hard Money Lending | Low | ~ 8—12% | Moderate | High |
| Private Equity/ Startups | Very Low | Highly variable | Low | Very High |

This table only scratches the surface, but it should give you a good sense of the many alternative investment opportunities available. It's also worth noting that the figures above are broad historical ranges, not guarantees or expected returns.

So what does this actually look like in practice? I've laid out dozens of different investment types, but how do you put it all together? There's no *right* answer, but here's a look at my current net worth breakdown:

- Index Funds (41%)
- Real Estate (34%)
- Business Equity (13%)
- Cash (10%)
- Crypto (2%)

Index funds and real estate, the most tried and true of the bunch, make up about 75% of my portfolio. Another 13% of my net worth is in the businesses I own. Only 2% is invested in crypto, primarily Bitcoin and Ethereum. And I'm holding a higher-than-usual cash balance right now because we're planning to build a new house. Normally, that number would be much lower.

You don't need to copy my portfolio exactly. This is simply what I'm invested in—nothing fancy or complicated, just assets we've already covered in this book. I didn't build wealth by making risky bets. I did it by consistently focusing on the gap between my income and expenses, then investing that gap into proven assets over time.

## Invest in Alternatives Wisely

Alternative investments can spice up your portfolio, but they shouldn't be the main course. A general rule of thumb: keep them to under 10% of your net worth unless you're truly an expert in the space.

Consider it your "fun money" or speculative bucket in your journey to FI. Track it separately. And remember, if it goes to zero, it shouldn't derail your financial independence plan. During my own FI journey, less than 3% of my assets were in alternative investments.

I've seen far too many people learn this the hard way by risking everything on one speculative bet. I've seen people who went all-in on crypto during a bull run, only to watch their portfolio crash 80% overnight. Others have bought brick-and-mortar businesses without doing proper due diligence, only to discover the seller had inflated earnings or left behind hidden debts. And even in the startup world, people have invested $10K or more into "the next big thing" only to watch the company fold six months later.

And the horror stories don't stop there. I've seen folks max out credit cards to buy into a hot NFT project, only to be left with digital assets no one wanted six months later. Others took out HELOCs to buy a local business, thinking it would run itself, but ended up overwhelmed and in debt when they realized it was a full-time job. One aspiring investor sunk their entire emergency fund into a coin they heard about on Reddit, hoping it would multiply by 100 (it didn't).

These aren't cautionary tales to scare you off—they're reminders that if something sounds too good to be true, it probably is. You're probably not going to be the next crypto millionaire, your cousin doesn't have the "secret stock" that's going to multiply by a thousand this year, and no business will magically run itself after you buy it.

Smart investors still experiment, but they do it from a position of financial strength, not desperation. Alternative investments can absolutely work, but they should never be your plan A.

## Call to Action: Explore Alternatives

Take some time to explore the alternative investments we covered in this chapter and see if any make sense for your portfolio. Before jumping in, ask yourself:

- Do I truly understand this investment?

- Can I afford to lose this money?

- Am I chasing shiny objects or playing the long game?

Diversification is smart, but focus is powerful. Build your financial foundation first—then explore from a position of strength.

# CHAPTER 14

# TAX OPTIMIZATION - RETIREMENT ACCOUNTS

*"The avoidance of taxes is the only intellectual pursuit that carries any reward."*

— JOHN MAYNARD KEYNES

Taxes might not be exciting, but they're one of the most powerful levers you can pull on your path to financial independence. The more income you keep by legally reducing your taxes, the faster you'll reach your goals. This chapter isn't about loopholes or shady tricks. It's about understanding how the system works and learning to use it to your advantage.

## Why Taxes Matter for FI

Every dollar you save on taxes is a dollar you can invest, or use to buy back your time. And the sooner you understand the tax code, the more strategic you can be with how you earn, save, and invest.

Even though taxes are one of the largest expenses most people have, the average person spends just 2.3 hours per year on tax planning. Most people focus on basic filing and compliance, but very few spend time on strategic planning—the kind that can dramatically change your take-home pay, especially if you follow the income-boosting strategies from earlier in this book.

Some of these moves might seem insignificant—like clicking the right button in your investment account or choosing between a Roth and a Traditional option—but those small, five-second decisions can have massive ripple effects over time.

Let's look at an example. Tom and Monique both earn $150,000 per year. The only difference is that Monique spends a little time each year optimizing her taxes, while Tom does not. As a result, Tom pays $10,000 more in taxes each year than Monique. This continues for 30 years.

If Monique invests that extra $10,000 each year and earns an 8% return, she'll end up with $1,132,379 more than Tom. All from a bit of strategic tax planning each year.

Hopefully, you're convinced that tax optimization matters. Let's keep going.

## Understand Your Brackets

Tax brackets are one of the most misunderstood parts of the U.S. tax system. You've probably heard someone say "I'm in the 25% tax bracket," and assume that means *all* of their income is taxed at 25%. Wrong. Or maybe you've heard someone say, "I don't want to make more money because it'll push me into the next tax bracket." Also wrong.

Here's how it actually works: Think of tax brackets as layers. Each layer of your income is taxed at a different rate, and only the money *within* that bracket is taxed at that rate. Once you earn more than a bracket allows, the *next dollar* spills over into the next bracket—getting taxed at that higher rate, not all of your income.

Let's look at the 2026 tax brackets, and then I'll walk through a real example to make it crystal clear.

| Tax Rate | Single Filers (Taxable Income) | Married Filing Jointly (Taxable Income) | Head of Household (Taxable Income) |
|---|---|---|---|
| 10% | $0 – $12,400 | $0 – $24,800 | $0 – $17,700 |
| 12% | $12,401 – $50,400 | $24,801 – $100,800 | $17,701 – $67,450 |
| 22% | $50,401 – $105,700 | $100,801 – $211,400 | $67,451 – $105,700 |
| 24% | $105,701 – $201,775 | $211,401 – $403,550 | $105,701 – $201,775 |
| 32% | $201,776 – $256,225 | $403,551 – $512,450 | $201,751 – $256,200 |
| 35% | $256,226 – $640,600 | $512,451 – $768,700 | $256,201 – $640,600 |

| 37% | Over $640,600 | Over $768,700 | Over $640,600 |
| --- | --- | --- | --- |

Tip: Search "tax brackets [your year]" to get the latest numbers.

Let's say a single filer earns $150,000 in taxable income in 2026. Here's how that income breaks down across the tax brackets:

- The first $12,400 is taxed at 10%.

- The next $12,401 to $50,400 is taxed at 12%.

- The next $50,401 to $105,700 is taxed at 22%.

- And the final $44,300 ($150,000 – $105,700) is taxed at 24%.

So yes, this person is "in" the 24% tax bracket, but only $44,300 of their income is actually taxed at that rate. The rest is taxed at the lower rates in the earlier brackets.

A more useful number to look at is the effective tax rate— essentially the weighted average of the tax you pay across all brackets. In this example, the person earning $150,000 pays roughly an effective tax rate of 19.1%, even though they're "in" the 24% bracket. And if their income were $205,000 instead, they'd be "in" the 32% bracket, but only the top $3,224 of their income (*$205,000 - $201,776*) would be taxed at that rate.

The U.S. tax system is progressive. You only pay higher rates on the income that crosses into the next bracket, not your entire income. Knowing the difference between your tax brackets and effective tax rate helps you make smarter decisions about

Roth vs. Traditional contributions, when to realize capital gains, and more.

## Tax-Advantaged Accounts

First, let's talk about tax-advantaged accounts. This is the five-second, click-of-a-button kind of tax savings I mentioned earlier. Remember the plant-and-garden analogy? Now we're talking about the types of gardens you'll want to use to hold your plants (your investments).

Using these accounts versus not using them can mean tens of thousands of dollars in potential tax savings each year. These accounts are specifically designed to help you save for retirement, and they come with serious tax perks.

Before we dive in, let's make sure you fully understand the difference between a Traditional and a Roth account, since many of the accounts we'll discuss have both options.

A Traditional account is funded with pre-tax dollars. When you contribute, you lower your taxable income for that year, but you'll pay taxes later when you withdraw the money in retirement.

A Roth account, on the other hand, is funded with after-tax dollars. You don't get a tax break today, but your money grows tax-free, and you won't owe a penny in taxes when you withdraw it in retirement (as long as you meet the withdrawal requirements).

If that still sounds a little confusing, let's look at an example.

Tony and Alexa both earn $100,000 in taxable income.

- Tony contributes $5,000 to a Traditional account (401(k), IRA, etc.). Because Traditional accounts are pre-tax, his contribution reduces his taxable income to $95,000 (*$100,000 - $5,000*).

- Alexa contributes $5,000 to a Roth account (401(k), IRA, etc.). Because Roth accounts are after-tax, her taxable income remains $100,000, and she doesn't get an immediate deduction.

They both retire 30 years later and begin withdrawing from their accounts.

When Tony withdraws $50,000 from his Traditional (pre-tax) accounts, the entire $50,000 is treated as taxable income because he never paid taxes on those contributions up front. Depending on his tax bracket, he'll owe income taxes on those withdrawals.

When Alexa withdraws $50,000 from her Roth (after-tax) accounts, that money comes out completely tax-free—since she already paid taxes when she contributed (assuming she's over age 59½). No additional income tax is owed.

Here's how that looks side-by-side:

| Feature | Traditional Account | Roth Account |
| --- | --- | --- |
| **Contributions** | Made with pre-tax dollars | Made with after-tax dollars |
| **Tax impact today** | Lowers taxable income now | No change to taxable income |
| **Growth** | Tax-deferred | Tax-free |
| **Withdrawals** | Taxed as ordinary income | Completely tax-free (if qualified) |
| **Best for** | People who expect to be in a lower tax bracket later | People who expect to be in a higher tax bracket later |

At the simplest level, choosing between a Traditional and a Roth comes down to this question: *"Do I expect to be in a higher tax bracket now or later?"* There are a lot of variables that influence this—like when you plan to retire, future government tax policy, and your expected income in retirement—but that's the right way to think about it.

Now that you have a clearer understanding of how Traditional and Roth accounts work, let's dive into the different account types available, how to use them, and who they're best for.

*401(k)*

This is a type of retirement account offered by the majority of companies. In 2026, the maximum amount you can contribute as an employee is $24,500 a year (or $32,500 a year if you're age 50 or older). Most employers offer both a Traditional and a Roth option.

**Pros**: Offers major tax advantages, potential employer matching (free money), and high contribution limits—all while allowing your investments to grow tax-deferred or tax-free.

**Cons**: Limited investment choices, penalties for early withdrawals, and reduced flexibility since your money is tied up until retirement (well, not entirely true).

*Solo 401(k)*

This is a retirement account for self-employed individuals or business owners with no employees (other than a spouse). It combines the best parts of a Traditional 401(k) and an IRA, offering both employee and employer contributions. In 2026, the total contribution limit is $72,000 a year; catch-up and employer contributions can raise your max above that depending on plan specifics.

**Pros:** Very high contribution limits, can be set up as either Traditional or Roth, and allows you to shelter a large portion of your self-employment income from taxes. It also lets you take loans from the account if needed.

**Cons:** More complex to set up and administer than a SEP IRA, limited to businesses with no employees, and subject to required minimum distributions (RMDs—mandatory withdrawals that begin later in life) if using the Traditional version.

*403(b)*

This is a type of retirement account offered by public schools, nonprofits, and certain government organizations. In 2026, the maximum employee contribution is $24,500 a year (or $32,500 a year if you're age 50 or older). Like a 401(k), most 403(b) plans offer both a Traditional and a Roth option.

**Pros**: Similar benefits to a 401(k)—tax advantages, potential employer matching, and high contribution limits—with the added perk of lower fees in some nonprofit plans.

**Cons**: Fewer investment choices compared to most 401(k)s, penalties for early withdrawals, and limited flexibility since your money is intended for long-term retirement use.

*457(b)*

This is a retirement account available to government employees and some nonprofit workers. It's similar to a 401(k) or 403(b), allowing you to contribute pre-tax or Roth dollars. In 2026, the contribution limit is $24,500 a year (or $32,500 a year if you're age 50 or older).

**Pros:** Offers tax advantages, high contribution limits, and unique flexibility—unlike other retirement accounts, you can withdraw funds penalty-free once you leave your job, even if you're under 59½. Ordinary income tax still applies to withdrawals.

**Cons:** Limited to certain employers, investment choices can be narrow, and if you withdraw funds while still employed, you'll typically face taxes and restrictions.

## *TSP*

This is a retirement account offered to federal employees and members of the military. In 2026, the maximum employee contribution is $24,500 a year (or $32,500 a year if you're age 50 or older). The TSP offers both Traditional and Roth options, along with a simple selection of low-cost index funds.

**Pros**: Extremely low fees, tax advantages, and automatic payroll contributions that make saving effortless. The TSP's simplicity and low costs make it one of the most efficient retirement plans available.

**Cons**: Limited investment options, penalties for early withdrawals, and less flexibility if you want to actively manage or diversify your investments beyond what's offered.

## *IRA*

This is an individual retirement account that you open on your own through a brokerage or financial institution. In 2026, you can contribute up to $7,500 per year (or $8,500 if you're age 50 or older). IRAs come in two main types—Traditional and Roth—and offer more control and investment flexibility than employer-sponsored plans.

**Pros**: Greater investment options, tax advantages, and the ability to choose between a Traditional (pre-tax) or Roth (post-tax) setup.

**Cons**: Lower contribution limits than a 401(k) or 403(b), potential penalties for early withdrawals, and income limits that may restrict Roth IRA eligibility for higher earners.

*SEP IRA*

This is a retirement account designed for self-employed individuals and small business owners. It works a lot like a Traditional IRA, but with much higher contribution limits. In 2026, you can contribute up to 25% of your yearly net earnings from self-employment, capped at $72,000. Contributions are tax-deductible, grow tax-deferred, and are taxed as ordinary income when withdrawn in retirement.

**Pros:** Simple to set up, high contribution limits, and tax-deductible contributions that reduce your taxable income today. It's a great option for freelancers or small business owners who want to save aggressively for retirement.

**Cons:** No Roth option, no catch-up contributions for those over 50, and if you have employees, you're generally required to contribute the same percentage of pay for them as you do for yourself.

*HSA*

This is a tax-advantaged account designed to help you save for medical expenses, but it can also double as a stealth retirement account. To qualify, you must be enrolled in a high-deductible health plan (HDHP). In 2026, the contribution limit is $4,400 a year for individuals and $8,750 a year for families, with an extra $1,000 catch-up contribution if you're 55 or older.

**Pros:** Triple tax advantage—contributions are tax-deductible, growth is tax-free, and withdrawals for qualified medical expenses are tax-free. Unused funds roll over each year, and after age 65, you can withdraw for any reason (though non-medical withdrawals are taxed like a Traditional IRA).

**Cons:** Must have a high-deductible health plan to qualify, non-medical withdrawals before age 65 incur taxes and a 20% penalty, and investing options can be limited depending on the provider.

There are also other tax-advantaged accounts designed for education savings—like 529 plans, ESA accounts, and custodial accounts such as UTMAs and UGMAs. If you're saving for a child's future, those can be great options to explore. But since this book is focused on helping *you* retire as quickly as possible, I'll let you dig into those on your own.

I know that was a lot of information at once, but my goal is to give you the full menu of options so you can craft your own perfect retirement recipe.

Let's recap:

| Account Type | Who It's For | 2026 Contribution Limit | Tax Treatment | Early Withdrawal Rules | Notable Benefits |
|---|---|---|---|---|---|
| **401(k)** | Employees of private companies | $24,500 ($32,500 if 50+) | Traditional (pre-tax) or Roth (after-tax) | 10% penalty before 59½ | Employer match, high limits |
| **Solo 401(k)** | Self-employed with no employees | Up to $72,000 ($80,000 if 50+) | Traditional or Roth | 10% penalty before 59½ | Combines employee + employer contributions |

| 403(b) | Public school & nonprofit employees | $24,500 ($32,500 if 50+) | Traditional or Roth | 10% penalty before 59½ | Similar to 401(k), sometimes lower fees |
|---|---|---|---|---|---|
| 457(b) | Government & some nonprofit workers | $24,500 ($32,500 if 50+) | Traditional or Roth | No penalty if you leave your employer | Penalty-free withdrawals after separation |
| TSP | Federal employees & military | $24,500 ($32,500 if 50+) | Traditional or Roth | 10% penalty before 59½ | Extremely low fees, simple fund options |
| IRA | Anyone with earned income | $7,500 ($8,500 if 50+) | Traditional or Roth | 10% penalty before 59½ | Full control over investments |
| SEP IRA | Self-employed & small-business owners | Up to 25% of income (max $72,000) | Traditional only | 10% penalty before 59½ | Simple setup, high limits |
| HSA | Individuals with HDHP coverage | $4,300 (individual) / $8,550 (family) + $1,000 catch-up (55+) | Pre-tax contributions, tax-free growth & withdrawals for medical use | 20% penalty + taxes if non-medical before 65 | Triple tax advantage, flexible in retirement |

If you have a 401(k) or similar plan, an IRA, and an HSA, you can contribute at least $36,400 to tax-advantaged accounts in 2026—and possibly more depending on your age.

Let's walk through a simple example. Imagine you're 25, single, and earning $100,000 per year at your day job. In 2026, you can contribute $24,500 to your 401(k), $7,500 to an IRA, and $4,400 to an HSA—for a total of $36,400 invested in tax-advantaged accounts. If you have a nice employer who offers a 5% employer match, you're now looking at $5,000 extra in your 401(k) from the employer side, which brings your total in tax-advantaged accounts to $41,400.

If your goal is to invest most of your money in the stock market, doing so through tax-advantaged accounts is usually your best move. Now that you understand most of the account types and benefits, let's walk through how to prioritize and structure your retirement contributions in a way that actually makes sense, along with a few more advanced strategies if you're a real go-getter.

## Retirement Contributions

The thing about retirement accounts is that you can't go back in time and take advantage of them later, so the best time to use them is now. It'd be amazing if you could "backfill" your IRA or 401(k) with $100,000 to make up for past years you didn't contribute, but unfortunately, that's not how it works. You can only contribute up to the annual limit.

The good news? Investments compound fast. If you start maxing out an IRA today—$7,500 per year for the next 30 years—without even factoring in future contribution increases, you'd end up with about $849,000, assuming an 8% annual return. Not bad for something you can automate once and forget about.

Now, let's get tactical.

Each year, try to hit two key goals:

1. Max out your IRA (Roth or Traditional), and

2. Contribute enough to your 401(k) to get the full employer match.

Even if you're saving for a house, your kid's college fund, or another big milestone, make these two priorities. They're the easiest ways to grow your wealth and cut your tax bill at the same time. Once those are covered, you can decide what to do with any extra funds.

If you want to learn creative ways to get as much money as humanly possible into your retirement accounts, you'll love the next section on advanced contribution strategies. But if you'd rather use your extra cash to buy real estate or small businesses, don't worry—we'll cover that later.

## Advanced Contribution Strategies

These contributions are *not* for beginners, and only one or two may be available to you, but they're things I wish I knew when I was getting started, so I decided to include them.

### Backdoor Roth IRA

If your income is too high to contribute directly to a Roth IRA, there's a simple workaround called the Backdoor Roth IRA.

This strategy lets you take advantage of tax-free growth even if you've passed the Roth income limits.

Here's how it works:

1.  Contribute up to the maximum allowed to a Traditional IRA ($7,500 in 2026). Since your income is too high to deduct this contribution, it's made after-tax.

2.  After the contribution clears, convert that money to a Roth IRA.

3.  Because you already paid taxes on the contribution, there's little to no additional tax owed—just tax on any small amount of growth between the contribution and conversion.

If you follow these steps carefully, you've essentially created a Roth IRA through the "back door."

A few things to keep in mind:

•   To use the Backdoor Roth cleanly, you generally want no pre-tax money in your Traditional IRA. If you do, the IRS's pro-rata rule kicks in and makes part of your conversion taxable.

•   Because of that, many people roll existing pre-tax IRA funds into a 401(k) first (if their plan allows it), effectively "clearing the deck" for the Backdoor Roth.

•   Once the conversion is complete, the money sits in a Roth IRA, where it grows completely tax-free, and qualified withdrawals in retirement are also tax-free.

If you're over the income limit for Roth contributions, this is one of the most effective ways to keep building your tax-free retirement bucket.

### Mega Backdoor Roth

If your employer allows it, a Mega Backdoor Roth lets you contribute after-tax dollars into your 401(k) beyond the normal limits, then roll them into a Roth account for tax-free growth.

Here's how it works:

In 2026, the total 401(k) contribution limit (including employee, employer, and after-tax contributions) is $72,000.

- You can contribute up to $24,500 as an employee.

- Your employer might match part of that—let's say $7,500.

- That still leaves about $40,000 of potential *after-tax* contribution space in this example. The exact amount of after-tax space depends on your employer's plan and matching formula.

If your plan allows in-service transfers, you can move that after-tax money into a Roth 401(k) or Roth IRA, where it will grow completely tax-free.

To make this work, your plan must support:

- After-tax contributions

- In-service transfers (or in-plan Roth conversions)

One quick message to your HR department could mean tens of thousands of additional dollars flowing into your retirement accounts each year. If you're already maxing out your regular 401(k) and still have money left to save, this is one of the most powerful, little-known strategies out there to supercharge your tax-free retirement bucket.

### Side Business Solo 401(k)

If you have self-employment income—even from a small side hustle—you can open a Solo 401(k). This account lets you contribute as both the "employee" and the "employer."

In 2026:

- You can contribute up to $24,500 as the employee.

- Then, as the employer, you can contribute up to 20–25% of your net self-employment income (depending on your business structure), with a combined total limit of $72,000.

- If you're age 50 or older, you can add an $8,000 catch-up contribution on top of the $72,000 limit, depending on plan structure.

Now here's where it gets really interesting.

Let's say you already have a 401(k) through your full-time job and you're maxing out your employee contributions there. You can still open a Solo 401(k) for your side business and make *employer* contributions from that income. Because your side hustle is technically a separate business, you're allowed to make these additional contributions.

You can even take it one step further. If your Solo 401(k) allows after-tax contributions and Roth conversions, you can convert those employer contributions into your Roth Solo 401(k)—basically creating your own version of a "Mega Backdoor Roth."

For example:

- You earn $30,000 in net self-employment income from your side business.

- You can contribute 25% of that ($7,500) as the employer portion into your Solo 401(k).

- Then, you convert that $7,500 into your Roth Solo 401(k), where it will grow completely tax-free.

If you open your Solo 401(k) with a flexible custodian, you can even invest in:

- Real estate

- Small businesses

- Crypto

- Other alternative assets

All inside a tax-free Roth shell. Used correctly, this strategy can significantly boost your tax-free retirement savings, especially if you already have a full-time job and want to put your side hustle income to work. Always check with a tax professional before setting this up to make sure your plan allows for after-tax contributions and in-plan conversions.

*Spousal IRA*

If one spouse doesn't have earned income, you can still help them build retirement savings through a Spousal IRA. This strategy lets a working spouse contribute to an IRA on behalf of a non-working spouse, effectively doubling how much your household can save each year.

Here's how it works:

- The working spouse must have enough earned income to cover both contributions.

- Each spouse can contribute up to $7,500 in 2026 (or $8,500 if age 50 or older).

- You can choose either a Traditional IRA (for tax-deferred growth) or a Roth IRA (for tax-free growth).

For example, if you earn $120,000 and your spouse isn't currently working, you can contribute $7,500 to your own Roth IRA and another $7,500 to a Roth IRA for your spouse—$15,000 total going toward tax-advantaged retirement savings.

This is a great way to balance long-term wealth building, especially for couples where one partner takes time off work to raise kids, switch careers, or go back to school. It helps keep both spouses' retirement accounts growing, even if only one person has a paycheck coming in.

*Defined Benefit (Cash Balance) Plans*

If you're a high earner or business owner looking to save *way* beyond 401(k) limits, a Defined Benefit Plan—also called a

Cash Balance Plan—can be an incredibly powerful tool. Think of it like creating your own personal pension.

Here's how it works:

- You (or your business) commit to contributing a set amount each year to fund a "promised" future retirement benefit.

- The exact contribution limit depends on your age, income, and plan setup—but it can range anywhere from $50,000 to well over $300,000 per year depending on age, income, and plan design.

- Contributions are tax-deductible for the business and grow tax-deferred until retirement.

For example, a 50-year-old business owner earning $300,000 could contribute $200,000 or more annually, lowering taxable income and accelerating retirement savings. Contribution limits rise with age, which is why these plans are especially powerful for older high earners.

These plans are especially popular among doctors, attorneys, consultants, and other high-income professionals with consistent cash flow. You can even combine a Defined Benefit Plan with a 401(k) for even more tax savings.

They do come with more complexity and costs than a standard retirement plan, and you'll need an actuary or plan administrator to set it up and manage it properly. But if you're earning a high income and want to shelter more money from taxes, this strategy can be a game-changer.

# Building Your Retirement Account Strategy

Your retirement account strategy will depend on your specific situation. I didn't use every strategy mentioned above, but several played a key role in my own FI journey. Since my income was too high to contribute to a Roth IRA directly, I used the Backdoor Roth IRA strategy to get around the limit. I also maxed out my Solo 401(k) (both employee and employer sides) using the Mega Backdoor Roth strategy, and maxed out my HSA.

Altogether, I was putting away over $60,000 per year into tax-advantaged accounts—the 2026 equivalent would be around $83,900. Today, I have a healthy portion of my net worth sitting in those accounts, quietly compounding for retirement. You might be wondering why I'd want to "tie up" so much money in retirement accounts when the goal is to retire early. For one, I'm living off cash flow from my digital products and real estate, so I don't need that money right now. And second, there are ways to access retirement accounts early without penalties—which we'll cover later.

One important thing to keep in mind—regardless of which retirement accounts you use—is *what* investments you place inside each account. Asset location matters.

For example, if you choose to allocate a small portion of your portfolio to more volatile investments (like crypto, penny stocks, or meme stocks), it often makes the most sense to hold those inside a Roth account rather than a taxable brokerage or a Traditional account. That way, if one of those bets really takes off, the gains can be withdrawn completely tax-free.

The same idea applies to stocks and bonds. Early in your journey, stocks will likely make up most of your portfolio since you're focused on growth. As you get closer to retirement—or begin dialing back work—you'll probably add more bonds to reduce volatility and increase stability.

Here's a simple rule of thumb for where to place each:

- Bonds often make the most sense in Traditional accounts. Bond income is taxed as ordinary income, so it's usually best to shelter it inside Traditional accounts like 401(k) s or IRAs.

- Put stocks in Roth and taxable accounts. Stocks tend to grow faster and are taxed more favorably, or not at all when held in a Roth account.

You probably won't own many bonds early on, but understanding this strategy now will make future portfolio decisions much easier when the time comes.

At the end of the day, you don't need fancy strategies to reach financial independence, but they can definitely help. I know plenty of people who retired before 30 without doing anything complicated. The key is to use what makes sense for your situation, and keep taking consistent action until you reach your desired goal.

## Call to Action: Set Up Retirement Accounts

Now that you understand how taxes actually work, take a moment to look at your own situation. Are you taking full advantage of the retirement accounts available to you?

If not, identify which ones apply and set up a system to start contributing. Putting your money in the right buckets can save you thousands in taxes every single year.

# CHAPTER 15

# TAX OPTIMIZATION - REAL ESTATE, BUSINESS, AND INCOME ENGINEERING

*"The tax code is a series of incentives
for certain kinds of behavior."*

— BILL BRADLEY

This chapter is a little more niche than the last one, but don't skip it just because you don't own rental properties or think you "don't have a business." There are strategies here that almost everyone can use. Even a small side hustle opens the door to powerful tax advantages. And income engineering—the art of legally structuring your income to minimize taxes—is something just about anyone can benefit from.

As you read, pick out what applies to you now, what might apply in the future, and what sparks your curiosity. You never know when one of these ideas could save you thousands down the road. Keep this chapter (and the previous one) bookmarked—you'll want to revisit them as your financial situation evolves.

## Real Estate Tax Benefits

Real estate isn't just about cash flow. It also comes with tax advantages. Last year, we earned just over $250,000 from our real estate investments and paid almost nothing in income taxes. Some investors own hundreds of properties, bring in millions in revenue, and still pay very little.

Before we dive into these strategies, there's one important concept to understand: active income vs. passive income in real estate. This isn't the same as the "active" and "passive" income we talked about earlier in the Income section. In this context, we're talking about how the IRS defines active and passive income specifically for real estate investors.

In the eyes of the IRS:

- **Active income** is money you earn from actively working—like running a business, flipping houses, or performing real estate services where you materially participate.

- **Passive income** comes from investments where you're not materially involved, such as owning rental properties managed by others or investing in syndications. Even though you earn income, you're not actively working in the business.

This distinction matters because, under normal circumstances, passive losses (like depreciation) can only offset passive income—not active income from your job or business. But some of the strategies in the next sections (like Real Estate Professional Status and the Short-Term Rental Loophole) can help you bridge that gap and use real estate losses to offset other types of income. Before we jump into the advanced stuff, let's take a step back and start with the basics.

*Deductible Expenses*

Real estate also comes with a long list of deductions that can drastically lower your taxable income. You can write off things like mortgage interest, property taxes, insurance, maintenance, repairs, and even property management fees. Basically, if it's a necessary expense to keep your property running, it's probably deductible.

For example, if your rental property brings in $18,000 per year and you spend $12,000 on qualified expenses, you're only taxed on the $6,000 profit. And that's before you even factor in depreciation, which can lower your taxable income even more. These deductions don't just save you money at tax time; they also boost your cash flow. The less you pay in taxes, the more money stays in your pocket to reinvest or use toward other financial goals.

And it's not just for full-time landlords. Even house hackers can benefit. If you rent out part of your home—say, a basement apartment or a spare bedroom—you can deduct a portion of your expenses based on the percentage of the property you're renting out. It's one of the few ways to turn your primary residence into both a home and an income-generating, tax-efficient asset.

## Depreciation

Depreciation is basically a tax break for property owners. The IRS lets you write off part of your property's value each year as if it's wearing out over time—even if it's actually going up in value. This helps lower your taxable income without you having to spend any money out of pocket.

**Formula**: Property value (excluding land) ÷ 27.5 years = annual depreciation

If you buy a $325,000 rental property and the land value is $50,000, you'd depreciate $275,000 over 27.5 years (don't ask me why the IRS picked 27.5 years—that's just how the rule works). That's $10,000 per year in depreciation in this example. If you made $10,000 in rental income, you could then subtract the $10,000 in depreciation, and your taxable income would be $0. That's how regular depreciation works.

But there's an even bigger opportunity called *bonus depreciation*. Normally, you'd spread your depreciation deductions out over 27.5 years, but with bonus depreciation, you can write off a large chunk of the property's value in the first year. This can create massive paper losses that offset other income, even though you didn't actually lose any money.

Using the same $325,000 rental property as an example, let me show you another strategy: a cost segregation study. This type of study is key for unlocking bonus depreciation. It breaks the property down into individual components—like appliances, flooring, cabinets, and certain plumbing or electrical systems. Instead of depreciating the entire building evenly over 27.5 years, the cost segregation study identifies which components wear out faster and allows them to be depreciated over much shorter timeframes.

With standard depreciation, you'd take the building value (excluding the $50,000 land value), divide the remaining $275,000 by 27.5 years, and end up with about $10,000 per year in depreciation to offset rental income. But with a cost segregation study, a portion of that value—say $100,000— might qualify as "short-lived" assets. Thanks to bonus depreciation, those components can often be written off immediately in the first year. The exact amount depends on the year the property is placed in service and current bonus depreciation rules.

That means if you earned $100,000 in rental income that year, you could potentially offset a large portion—or all—of it using cost segregation and bonus depreciation. This is one of the most powerful tools in real estate for reducing taxes and freeing up cash flow you can reinvest into additional properties or other income-producing assets.

That said, there's an important tradeoff to understand. If you sell a property where you've used bonus depreciation, you may owe depreciation recapture, which can result in a sizable tax bill. This strategy can be incredibly effective, but it's not something to implement blindly. Be sure to consult a qualified real estate CPA or tax professional before moving forward.

### 1031 Exchanges

A 1031 exchange is another powerful tax tool available to real estate investors. It lets you sell an investment property and defer paying capital gains taxes by reinvesting the profits into another "like-kind" property. In other words, instead of paying the IRS when you sell, you can roll those gains directly into your next deal and keep your money working for you.

Let's say you sell a rental property for a $100,000 gain. Normally, you'd owe capital gains taxes on that profit, but with a 1031 exchange, you can reinvest the full $100,000 into another investment property and pay no taxes today. Those taxes are deferred until you eventually sell a property without reinvesting.

The real magic is that you can repeat this process over and over—trading up from a small rental to a multi-unit property, then into commercial real estate, and so on—all while deferring taxes and compounding your gains along the way. Many investors use this strategy to build massive portfolios without ever triggering a taxable event.

To make this work, you need to follow the IRS's strict rules. You must identify your replacement property within 45 days of selling the old one and close within 180 days. Work with a qualified intermediary to make sure the transaction meets all requirements, because one missed detail can nullify the entire tax benefit.

Pro Tip: If you keep rolling your gains forward and eventually pass your properties down to your heirs, they receive what's called a *step-up in cost basis*. That means your deferred gains are completely wiped out when the property changes hands, and your heirs inherit it at today's market value—potentially avoiding decades of taxes altogether.

## Section 121 Exclusion

If you've lived in your property for at least two of the last five years before selling it, you may qualify for one of the most generous tax breaks in real estate. It's called the Section 121 Exclusion, and it lets you avoid paying capital gains taxes on a large portion of your profits when you sell your primary residence.

Here's how it works in 2026:

- If you're single, you can exclude up to $250,000 of capital gains.

- If you're married filing jointly, you can exclude up to $500,000.

For example, if you bought a home for $300,000, lived there for two years, and later sold it for $600,000, you could walk away with the entire $300,000 profit tax-free (if married).

And when the IRS says you must have "lived there for two years," those years don't have to be consecutive. For instance, you could buy a home in Florida, live there for one year, move to California for three years, then return to the Florida home and live there for another year. Because you lived in the property for two of the last five years, you'd still qualify for the Section 121 Exclusion.

This rule can also benefit house hackers—people who live in one part of a property while renting out the rest. As long as you meet the two-out-of-five-year residency requirement, you can exclude the capital gains on the portion of the home you personally lived in (excluding depreciation recapture, which is still taxable).

It's also worth noting that the Section 121 Exclusion is limited to once every two years.

*Real Estate Professional Status (REPS)*

If you've spent any time around real estate investors, you've probably heard people talk about Real Estate Professional Status, or "REPS." It's one of the most powerful tax designations in the entire tax code—but also one of the most misunderstood.

Here's why it's such a big deal: normally, rental income is considered passive by the IRS. That means you can't use real estate losses (like depreciation) to offset your active income (like a W-2 job, business income, or self-employment income). But if you qualify for Real Estate Professional Status, the game changes. Your real estate losses can offset your active income, which can dramatically reduce your tax bill.

To qualify, you (or your spouse) must meet two key requirements:

1. You spend more than 750 hours per year working in real estate activities (like managing properties, rehabs, or acquisitions).

2. Those hours must make up more than half of your total working time for the year.

If you're married, only one spouse needs to meet the REPS requirements for both of you to benefit from it on your joint tax return. Many investors also make a grouping election so all properties are treated as one activity.

Let's say one spouse works full-time as a real estate agent, investor, or property manager, and qualifies for REPS. The other spouse has a W-2 job making $150,000. If their real estate portfolio produces a $100,000 "loss" from depreciation and deductible expenses, that loss can offset $100,000 of W-2 income—potentially saving tens of thousands of dollars in taxes.

This is why so many financially independent couples strategically structure their work around REPS. One spouse leans into real estate full-time, while the other focuses on their career. It's an incredibly powerful way to accelerate wealth building and keep more of what you earn.

Just keep in mind: the IRS scrutinizes REPS claims closely. You'll need to keep detailed logs of your hours, tasks, and properties to prove you meet the requirements. But if you do, the tax savings can be life-changing.

Even if you or your spouse doesn't qualify for REPS, you can still use real estate to reduce your active income in other ways.

*The Short-Term Rental Loophole*

This strategy has become a favorite among investors looking to reduce their taxable income—especially those who don't qualify as full-time real estate professionals. It's often called the short-term rental loophole, and it allows you to use real estate losses (like depreciation) to offset your regular W-2 or business income.

Here's the gist: normally, rental real estate is considered *passive income* by the IRS, which means you can't use losses from rentals to offset *active income* (like your job or business). But short-term rentals are treated differently.

If your average guest stay is seven days or less (or under 30 days in certain cases), the IRS no longer classifies your rental as a traditional rental activity—it's considered a *business.* That means your losses, including depreciation and bonus depreciation, may offset other active income if you meet certain participation requirements.

To qualify, you need to materially participate in the business, which usually means:

- Spending 100 hours or more on the property annually, and

- Participating more than anyone else (you can't just hire a property manager to do everything).

Let's say you buy a short-term rental property and run it as an Airbnb. You actively manage bookings, handle guest communication, and oversee cleaning and maintenance. The property earns $60,000 in income and has $40,000 in expenses. Through a cost segregation study and bonus depreciation, you're able to take a $100,000 depreciation deduction.

On paper, that turns a $20,000 profit into an $80,000 tax loss ($60,000 – $40,000 – $100,000 = –$80,000). In the right situation, that loss may be used to offset W-2 income—potentially saving tens of thousands of dollars in taxes. It's a huge opportunity for active investors, but it's also one that the IRS watches closely. Keep excellent records of your time spent managing the property, and talk to a tax professional before implementing this strategy. When used correctly, the short-term rental loophole can dramatically reduce your tax bill and supercharge your path to financial independence.

Some investors use this loophole to capture the upfront tax benefits, then switch the property to a long-term rental after claiming bonus depreciation. This allows them to enjoy the massive first-year write-off while eventually making the property more passive—essentially getting the best of both worlds. If you're going to do this, make sure you have proper documentation and follow all applicable IRS guidelines.

As you've seen, real estate offers some of the most powerful tax advantages out there—from depreciation to 1031 exchanges—but it's not the only way to keep more of what you earn. If you run a business or have any kind of self-employment income, the tax code gives you even more opportunities to save. In fact, business owners have more flexibility with deductions, retirement contributions, and income structuring than almost anyone else.

So, now that we've covered how to minimize taxes through real estate, let's talk about how to do the same through your business or side hustle.

## Self-Employment & Business Taxes

Running a business—whether it's a full-time venture or a small side hustle—opens up a world of potential tax write-offs. Unlike W-2 employees, who have limited ability to deduct work-related expenses, business owners can deduct anything that's considered an "ordinary and necessary" expense for running their business.

Here's what that means:

- **Who qualifies:** Anyone earning self-employment or business income. This could include freelancing, real estate investing, selling digital products, consulting, or running a physical or online business.

- **What qualifies:** If an expense is directly related to earning business income and would be considered normal in your line of work, it likely qualifies. Think: laptops, marketing software, home office space, phone plans, internet, travel for client meetings, or professional services.

- **Mixed-use items:** If you use something for both personal and business reasons (like your car, phone, or computer), you can deduct the business-use portion.

Here's an easy rule of thumb: If the IRS showed up tomorrow, could you confidently say, *"This expense directly helped me earn money in my business"*? If yes, it's probably a legitimate deduction.

Remember, the tax code is basically a series of incentives. It rewards you for doing things the government wants to encourage—creating jobs, providing services, or building housing. The more you understand and use those incentives, the more control you gain over your tax bill.

Pro Tip: Proper bookkeeping and keeping a separate business bank account make this much easier. Not only will it simplify tax season, but it'll also help your accountant work their magic when it's time to file. I'll cover this in more detail shortly.

### Everyday Deductions

Let's start with the basics—the everyday write-offs that almost every business owner can take advantage of. These are the easy wins that add up fast.

- **Home Office Deduction:** If you have a dedicated space in your home used exclusively and regularly for business, you can deduct a portion of your rent, utilities, and internet based on business use. The simplified method lets you write off $5 per square foot (up to 300 sq. ft.).

- **Vehicle Expenses:** If you drive for business purposes, you can deduct either your actual expenses (gas, maintenance, insurance) or use the standard mileage rate (which changes each year). Keep a mileage log or use an app— it's worth it.

- **Everyday Tools:** Laptops, software, subscriptions, marketing platforms, and even part of your cell phone bill can be written off if you use them for business.

- **Travel & Meals:** Flights, lodging, and 50% of meals for legitimate business trips are deductible. Keep receipts and document the purpose of each trip.

These small deductions might not seem like much individually, but together, they can make a huge difference in lowering your taxable income.

*Bigger Business Deductions*

As your business grows, so do your opportunities for bigger deductions. These take a little more planning but can lead to serious tax savings.

- **Startup Costs:** You can deduct up to $5,000 in startup expenses your first year in business—things like website design, equipment, or legal fees.

- **Education & Training:** Courses, certifications, conferences, or books that improve your skills or grow your business are deductible.

- **Health Insurance Premiums:** If you're self-employed, you can often deduct your health insurance premiums (and your family's).

- **Depreciation & Section 179:** Large purchases like equipment, furniture, or computers can be deducted all at once under Section 179, instead of being depreciated over several years.

These are the kinds of deductions that can turn a five-figure tax bill into a much smaller one.

*Advanced Strategies*

Once you're earning more, it's time to start thinking like a CFO. These advanced strategies can help you optimize your structure and minimize taxes even further.

- **Choosing the Right Business Structure (The S-Corp Advantage):** If you're currently operating as a single-member LLC or sole proprietor and your business is consistently earning more than about $50,000 per year in profit, it might make sense to elect S-Corp status.

  Here's why: when you're self-employed, you pay self-employment tax (about 15.3%) on all your business profits. But with an S-Corp, you can split your income between a reasonable salary (which is taxed normally) and distributions (which aren't subject to self-employment tax).

  For example, if your business makes $100,000 in profit, you might pay yourself a $60,000 salary and take the remaining $40,000 as distributions—potentially saving over $6,000 in taxes.

  This strategy does come with extra paperwork and payroll costs, so it's not for everyone. But once your business reaches a certain size, it can be a game-changer.

- **Qualified Business Income (QBI) Deduction:** If you operate as a pass-through entity—such as a sole proprietorship, LLC, or S-corp—you may be eligible to deduct up to 20% of your qualified business income. This deduction reduces your taxable income and can save thousands of dollars each year.

There are income thresholds (which adjust annually for inflation) and additional limitations for certain service-based businesses, but many entrepreneurs still qualify. With thoughtful income planning—sometimes including an S-corp structure—the deduction can remain available even as income grows. This is a complex area of the tax code, so it's best implemented with the help of a knowledgeable CPA.

- **Hiring Family Members:** Paying your kids or spouse for legitimate work in your business can shift income into lower tax brackets while still keeping money in the family. For example, paying your child $12,000 per year for actual work—like handling social media, shipping products, or helping with admin—means they owe no income tax (if it's under the standard deduction), and you get a business deduction for the expense.

  If your business is a sole proprietorship or single-member LLC (not an S-corp), you don't even need to pay payroll taxes on your kids under 18. This makes it one of the most efficient (and totally legal) ways to move money from your business to your household tax-free.

These strategies require more effort up front, but they can save you thousands each year as your business grows. Again, take or leave any or all of these. I'm not trying to overwhelm you here. I just want to give you a menu of options to choose from for your own tax situation.

## *Bookkeeping & Recordkeeping*

When I first started side hustling and running businesses, my bookkeeping was an absolute mess. I ran multiple businesses through my personal bank account and credit card, then banged my head against a wall at tax time trying to properly sort every single transaction.

Learn from my mistakes and keep your business and personal finances completely separate. Use a dedicated business bank account and credit card, and track your income and expenses throughout the year. Whether you use software like QuickBooks, Wave, or even a simple spreadsheet, the key is consistency.

Save receipts, keep digital backups, and jot quick notes about what each expense was for. If you ever get audited, having clean, organized records turns a nightmare into a five-minute conversation. Good bookkeeping doesn't just make tax season easier—it helps you understand how your business is performing, plan smarter, and make better decisions year-round.

It's also important to remember that self-employed people are responsible for paying taxes quarterly instead of having them automatically withheld. A good rule of thumb is to set aside 25–30% of your profits for taxes so you're never caught off guard. I learned that lesson the hard way, too.

Good bookkeeping makes taking advantage of all the tax strategies we just covered much easier. And to be clear, I don't expect you to implement all of them right away. The goal is awareness. You might only use one or two today, but knowing what's possible helps you make smarter decisions as your income grows and your situation becomes more complex. Once you start learning how to intentionally control your income, though, that's when things start to get really interesting.

## Income Engineering and Capital Gains Taxes

A common strategy used by people on the path to financial independence—and even by those who've already achieved it—is something called income engineering. This involves making intentional decisions about how much income you actually "show" on paper each year. By strategically controlling your taxable income, you can unlock specific tax advantages and opportunities that help you accelerate your journey to financial freedom.

Before we dive into those strategies, it's important to understand that not all income is taxed the same way. That's where capital gains tax comes in. Capital gains tax and income tax both apply to money you earn, but they cover different types of income. Income tax is what you pay on your job earnings, business income, or side hustles. Capital gains tax, on the other hand, applies when you sell an investment (like stocks or real estate) for more than you paid for it.

The main difference comes down to timing and rate. Income tax is typically higher and hits you every year you earn money, while capital gains tax is usually lower and only applies when you sell an investment for a profit. In fact, the government rewards long-term investors with lower tax rates for holding investments longer than a year.

Here's how long-term capital gains are taxed in 2026:

| Capital Gains Tax Rate | Single Filers (Taxable Income) | Married Filing Jointly (Taxable Income) | Head of Household (Taxable Income) |
|---|---|---|---|
| 0% | $0 – $49,450 | $0 – $98,900 | $0 – $66,200 |
| 15% | $49,451 – $545,500 | $98,901 – $613,700 | $66,201 – $579,600 |
| 20% | Over $545,500 | Over $613,700 | Over $579,600 |

Tip: Search "capital gains tax [your year]" to get the latest numbers.

For something to be considered a long-term capital gain, it must be held for at least one year before you sell it. If you sell it sooner, it's considered a short-term capital gain and is taxed at your regular income tax rate. Holding investments for more than a year usually means paying lower taxes than you would on ordinary income.

With some strategic income engineering, you may be able to realize capital gains at a 0% tax rate (or at least a lot of them). This opens the door for powerful moves like capital gains harvesting, Roth conversions, and more.

*Capital Gains Harvesting*

Capital gains harvesting is a strategy that takes advantage of periods of low income. During these windows—such as a sabbatical or early retirement—you may be able to sell investments at a gain and pay 0% in capital gains taxes.

If your taxable income falls below a certain threshold (for 2026, that's about $98,900 for married couples filing jointly), your long-term capital gains tax rate is 0%. That means you can sell appreciated investments—like stocks or index funds—lock in the gains, and immediately buy them back without paying any taxes. This effectively resets your cost basis (the price you originally paid for the investment). So later on, when you do sell those investments in a higher-income year, you'll owe taxes on a smaller gain.

Let's say you bought $20,000 of VTSAX a few years ago, and it's now worth $35,000. If you sell it during a low-income year while you're in the 0% capital gains bracket, you pay zero in taxes on that $15,000 gain. Then, you can turn around and rebuy the same investment at $35,000—meaning your new cost basis is $35,000. If you later sell at $50,000, you'll only owe taxes on that $15,000 increase instead of $30,000.

Capital gains harvesting is like tax-free housekeeping for your portfolio. It's especially powerful during career transitions, sabbaticals, early retirement, or any year where your taxable income dips. You're taking advantage of the low-income year *intentionally* to save thousands in future taxes.

### Roth Conversions

Another powerful move to make in low-income years is a Roth conversion. This strategy lets you move money from a

Traditional IRA or 401(k) (which is tax-deferred) into a Roth IRA (which grows and can be withdrawn tax-free).

When you convert funds from a Traditional account to a Roth, you'll owe income tax on the amount you convert. So, if your taxable income is unusually low, you can convert a chunk of your Traditional balance to a Roth while staying in a low tax bracket. You're essentially prepaying your taxes at a discount.

Let's say you're single, and after deductions, your taxable income for the year is $30,000. You could choose to convert additional money from a Traditional IRA to a Roth IRA—filling up the remainder of your current tax bracket without spilling into the next one. You'll pay ordinary income tax on the converted amount now, but from that point forward, the money grows tax-free, and qualified withdrawals in retirement will never be taxed again.

Roth conversions are especially powerful for early retirees or anyone on the path to FI who plans to have several low-income years before Social Security, pensions, or required minimum distributions kick in. You can chip away at your Traditional accounts, fill up the lower tax brackets, and shift that money into a tax-free bucket for life.

Think of it as tax bracket optimization. You're intentionally controlling how much income to show in a given year—paying taxes when they're cheap instead of when they're expensive. If you put all your money into pre-tax accounts and don't convert strategically, you could get hit with huge Required Minimum Distributions (RMDs) later. Converting some funds to Roth in your 30s, 40s, or early 50s can help reduce that future tax bomb.

And here's where it gets even better: later in this book, we'll talk about how you can use a Roth Conversion Ladder to access that money before traditional retirement age without penalties. This one-two punch—strategic conversions now and structured withdrawals later—is one of the most powerful tools on the path to financial independence.

*Other Hidden Benefits of Low Income*

Low-income years aren't just about tax savings—they come with a few hidden perks too. Whether you're taking a mini-retirement, scaling back work, or retiring for good, these years can be surprisingly powerful if you plan ahead. Here are a few ways to use them to your advantage.

1. **Lower-Cost Health Insurance (ACA Subsidies)** - The Affordable Care Act offers premium tax credits for people with moderate or low incomes. If your household income drops within the qualifying range, your health insurance premiums can be drastically reduced—or even free in some cases. Planning your withdrawals or conversions around this can save you thousands each year.

2. **Financial Aid Opportunities** - If you have kids heading to college, your household income plays a major role in determining financial aid eligibility. A strategically low-income year (like after early retirement or a sabbatical) can result in better aid

packages, lower tuition costs, and expanded access to grants or scholarships.

3. **Student Loan Forgiveness** - If you or your spouse has federal student loans, a low-income year can dramatically lower your required monthly payment under income-driven repayment (IDR) plans. In some cases, your required payment can even drop to $0 while still counting toward forgiveness timelines.

I'm not the biggest fan of some of these strategies, but they're worth mentioning. Use your own moral compass to decide which low-income perks make sense for you. I only listed a few, but the truth is that intentionally showing low income can open the door to nearly every low-income benefit out there—and rarely is your net worth ever checked for eligibility.

Which leads perfectly into the final section of this chapter: when tax optimization goes too far.

## When Tax Optimization Goes Too Far

Have you ever heard the phrase "don't let the tax tail wag the investment dog"? It means you shouldn't make every financial (or life) decision based solely on taxes. Sometimes, in the pursuit of ultimate efficiency, people end up optimizing themselves into misery.

Take entrepreneurs who move to Puerto Rico for its low-tax incentives. On paper, it sounds incredible—massive tax savings and more money in your pocket. But the catch is that you have to spend at least half the year there to qualify. Many people make the move, only to realize that uprooting their lives, relationships, and routines wasn't worth the slightly smaller tax bill. Now, if you genuinely want to move somewhere with lower taxes—like going from California to Texas—by all means, do it. That's lifestyle design. But making major life decisions purely to save money on taxes rarely ends well.

I've also seen people start businesses or dive into real estate only because they heard it came with tax advantages. Only once they're neck deep do they realize they hate it because it drains their time, energy, and happiness. Sure, they saved on taxes, but they paid a much higher price elsewhere.

The point is this: tax optimization is a tool, not a religion. It's meant to support your goals, not dictate them. If a strategy adds stress, limits your freedom, or makes life less enjoyable, it's probably not the right one for you. Remember, the goal of financial independence isn't to owe the government nothing. It's to buy back your time and design a life you love. Sometimes that means paying a little more in taxes and sleeping better at night.

## Call to Action: Improve Your Tax Strategy

I don't expect you to use everything from the last two chapters, but there's almost certainly *something* you can improve. Where can you simplify, automate, or optimize? Choose one or two tax strategies and actually put them into motion.

Tax optimization isn't about avoiding taxes—it's about understanding the rules and using them to your advantage. The less money you lose to taxes, the more you can invest, and the faster you'll reach financial independence.

# SECTION 5

# EARLY RETIREMENT

# CHAPTER 16

# ARE WE THERE YET?

*"There is no single formula for success. There are many paths, and each person must find their own."*

— JIM ROHN

When most people think of retirement, they picture an age: 65. But when you step into the world of financial independence, you realize there are a lot more options on the table. You realize that you don't have to wait until some magical age to start living life on your own terms. Instead, you can design a retirement plan that fits your lifestyle, values, and ambitions.

In this chapter, we'll explore the most common flavors of early retirement. Some are stepping stones, others are end goals, but all of them offer more freedom, control, and flexibility than the standard 40-year career. You'll also find examples using real numbers to help you visualize what each path could look like.

Let's break down the seven most common early retirement models—each with a different path to freedom.

## Mini-Retirements (Gap Years)

A mini-retirement is exactly what it sounds like—a temporary break from work that gives you time to travel, reflect, or recharge. Instead of saving everything for a distant retirement, you take short sabbaticals along the way. As my friend Jillian Johnsrud would say, you "retire often," versus just grinding until you reach financial freedom.

A mini-retirement can take a lot of different forms. You might save up a chunk of money, quit your job, and spend a year traveling through Southeast Asia. Or you could negotiate a 3–6 month sabbatical and use the time to hike, read, or dive into a passion project you've been putting off. The goal is simply to buy yourself time.

**The Numbers:** If your lifestyle costs $4,000 per month, a one-year mini-retirement requires around $48,000 in savings (plus a buffer). You can adjust that number based on the length of your mini-retirement.

**Pros:**

- You get a taste of freedom without waiting decades.
- Great way to reset your goals and priorities.

**Cons:**

- You'll need to pause investing or draw down savings temporarily.

- Harder to re-enter certain industries after a long break.

**Next Steps:** If you're thinking about taking a mini-retirement, start by figuring out *why* you want one. Are you craving adventure, time with family, space to think, or just a break from burnout? Clarity on your purpose will guide how long your break should be, how much you'll need to save, and what your time off will look like.

Next, run the numbers. Estimate your monthly spending, multiply it by however many months you want off, and add a small buffer. You don't need a million dollars to take a mini-retirement. You just need enough to cover expenses and buy yourself time. As part of that planning, make sure you account for health insurance. Before you quit, explore plans on HealthCare.gov, review any continuation options through your employer, or join your spouse's plan if that's available.

If you have a steady job, see if you can negotiate an unpaid sabbatical before quitting entirely. Some companies are surprisingly flexible if you've built goodwill. If you're self-employed, you might automate parts of your business, line up freelance projects for when you return, or build a small cash cushion first.

You can also "test drive" a mini-retirement with a shorter break—like a one-month trial run—to see how it feels financially and emotionally. It's usually less of a shock to your boss, and it gives you a chance to figure out how you'd spend a longer mini-retirement down the road.

This strategy is best for people who want to explore or recharge without fully committing to early retirement. A mini-retirement gives you space to reset, rethink, and come back more focused—and sometimes, it's the spark that shows you what kind of life you truly want to build next.

## Coast FI

Coast FI is a great model if you've already done the hard work early on and want to ease off the gas pedal. It happens when you've already invested enough that—if left to grow untouched—it will fully fund your traditional retirement. From here, you just need to earn enough to cover your current expenses—no more aggressive saving required.

Imagine that you're 30 and have $200,000 invested. At an 8% average return, that grows to almost $3 million by age 65—enough to retire comfortably for many people. Now, you only need to earn enough to fund your lifestyle, not to keep saving for it.

**The Numbers:** Use an investment calculator to project your current portfolio to your traditional retirement age. If the future value meets (or exceeds) your FI number, congrats—you can coast.

**Pros:**

- You can stop saving and just cover your expenses.

- More freedom to take lower-stress or more meaningful work.

**Cons:**

- Still dependent on active income.

- Slower net worth growth compared to continuing to save aggressively.

**Next Steps:** If you think you're close to Coast FI, start by running your numbers. Use an online compound interest calculator to project your current portfolio to your target retirement age. Play with different return rates and ages to see what the future could look like. The goal is to find that sweet spot where your investments, left alone, can grow to your financial independence number without any new contributions.

Once you've confirmed that you've hit Coast FI, it's time to rethink how you want to spend your time. Do you want to switch to a lower-stress job? Take a pay cut to pursue more meaningful work? Or maybe travel more, start a business, or work seasonally? The beauty of Coast FI is that you've already done the heavy lifting—you've built the snowball. Now you just need to keep it from melting.

It's also worth revisiting your budget and ensuring your current income comfortably covers your lifestyle and any short-term goals. You don't need to stop saving entirely, but the pressure's off. Every dollar you earn beyond your living expenses is just a bonus.

Most people underestimate how freeing it feels to reach this point. Coast FI is proof that financial independence doesn't have to be an all-or-nothing finish line. It can be a smoother, slower glide toward freedom.

## Barista FI

Barista FI is the middle ground between traditional employment and financial independence—a flexible lifestyle where your investments cover part of your expenses, and a part-time or lower-stress job covers the rest.

Many people use Barista FI as a bridge between full-time work and early retirement. You're not completely done working—you're just done working *for survival.*

For example, your investments might cover part of your expenses, and you make up the rest with a part-time or flexible job. Some people choose employers like Starbucks or Costco that offer health insurance to part-time employees, while drawing on their portfolio for the remainder.

**The Numbers:** Let's say you need $35,000 per year to live. If your portfolio covers $20,000, you're about 57 percent FI—you just need to make up the rest with income from a job you (hopefully) enjoy.

**Pros:**

- Maintains access to healthcare and other benefits through part-time work (depending on the job).

- Offers structure, social connection, and a sense of purpose without full-time pressure.

**Cons:**

- You still need to work, even if less.

- Requires balancing part-time income with investment withdrawals.

**Next Steps:** Start by exploring employers that offer benefits to part-time workers—many do. Starbucks, Costco, REI, and Trader Joe's are well-known examples, but universities, school districts, and some remote companies also provide health insurance or 401(k) matches for part-timers.

You can also look beyond traditional jobs. Freelancing, tutoring, consulting, or remote customer support can give you flexibility while still providing a small income stream.

Think of Barista FI as buying yourself time. You're covering your needs, maintaining key benefits, and letting your investments keep compounding in the background. This strategy is perfect for anyone who wants more freedom now, even if they're not fully financially independent yet.

## Lean FI

Lean FI means you've reached financial independence on a minimalist budget. You've saved enough to cover your essential expenses indefinitely, even if your lifestyle isn't luxurious. It's the leanest approach to freedom and is often used as a stepping stone toward a more comfortable version of FI later on.

For example, someone spending $25,000 per year would need a portfolio of roughly $750,000, based on the 4% rule (annual expenses × 25). To keep expenses *that* low, many people pursuing Lean FI move to lower-cost areas, live in a van or tiny home, or embrace a more minimalist lifestyle.

**The Numbers:** FI Number = Annual Expenses × 25 (e.g., $25,000 × 25 = $750,000)

**Pros:**

- You can reach financial independence much earlier.

- Forces you to be intentional with spending and appreciate simplicity.

**Cons:**

- Vulnerable to unexpected expenses or inflation.

- It can feel restrictive over time, especially if your values or lifestyle evolve.

**Next Steps:** Start by tracking your true annual expenses and identifying what's essential versus optional. This will give you a realistic sense of what your "Lean FI number" actually looks like.

Before committing fully, experiment with living lean. Try cutting your expenses to your projected Lean FI level for a few months and see how it feels. Can you live comfortably at that level, or does it start to feel too restrictive?

If it feels too tight, but you really want to stop working, it may be time to get creative. Many people living the Lean FI lifestyle use geoarbitrage—spending some or all of the year in a lower-cost area—to drastically reduce their expenses. I know several people who've moved to places in Asia or South America, where the cost of living is significantly lower. A $40,000-a-year lifestyle in the U.S. might cost closer to $10,000 in a place like Bali.

Lean FI is best suited for minimalists, digital nomads, or anyone who values time and freedom over comfort and luxury. If you're someone who can stretch a dollar and enjoys getting creative with how you live, this approach might be a great fit.

## Cash Flow FI

Cash Flow FI is when your passive income—from rentals, dividends, businesses, or other sources—covers all of your expenses. Unlike traditional retirement strategies that rely on withdrawing from a large investment portfolio, Cash Flow FI focuses on building income streams that pay you month after month.

This could look like:

- $3,000/month from rental properties

- $2,000/month from digital products

- $1,000/month from dividends

Once your passive—or mostly passive—cash flow consistently exceeds your monthly expenses, work becomes optional. Instead of selling investments to fund your lifestyle, you're living off income your assets produce.

If your goal is to reach financial independence as quickly as possible, Cash Flow FI is often the most direct path. With the right investments or systems in place, it's possible to reach FI in just a few years.

**The Numbers**: Start by calculating your spending—that's how much you need to earn each month in passive income. I recommend adding at least a 20% buffer to account for fluctuations or surprise expenses. For example, if you're spending $5,000 per month, aim for about $6,000 in mostly passive cash flow.

**Pros:**

- Doesn't require a massive investment portfolio.

- Can be reached in just a few years (or less).

**Cons:**

- Income can fluctuate or dry up unexpectedly.

- Requires ongoing management or occasional hands-on effort.

**Next Steps:** Identify where your strengths or interests could naturally generate recurring income. For some, that's real estate. For others, it's content creation, digital products, freelancing systems, or dividend investing.

The key is scalability and sustainability—build income streams that continue even when you're not constantly working. Begin with one stream, stabilize it, then add another. Think of it like constructing a portfolio of small, reliable passive income machines that run in the background.

It's also smart to diversify your cash flow sources. A mix of real estate, dividends, and business income creates resilience during market downturns or industry shifts.

Cash Flow FI is best for entrepreneurs, investors, and creators who want to retire early through *income* rather than *withdrawals*. It's an active approach to financial independence—one where you build freedom not by selling off assets, but by creating systems that pay you to live life on your terms.

## Traditional FI

Traditional FI is the classic path—earning, saving, and investing until your portfolio is large enough to cover all your living expenses for the rest of your life.

This is the version most people think of when they hear "financial independence." You build up a big enough nest egg that you can safely withdraw a small percentage each year (typically 4%), and live off your investments indefinitely.

So if you spend $60,000 per year, using the 4% rule, you need 25 times that amount invested, or about $1.5 million. Once you hit that number, your portfolio can theoretically support you forever—without needing to work another day.

**The Numbers:** FI Number = Annual Expenses × 25 (e.g., $60,000 × 25 = $1,500,000)

**Pros:**

- No ongoing work or income required once you reach your number.

- Easy to track your progress with a clear target.

**Cons:**

- Spending might turn into "Lean FI" during market downturns.

- It takes time and patience to build a large enough nest egg.

**Next Steps:** If Traditional FI is your goal, start by calculating your own FI number. Multiply your annual expenses by 25 (or 30 if you want to be extra conservative). That's your target.

Next, automate your investing so a percentage of every paycheck goes straight into low-cost index funds through your 401(k), IRA, or brokerage account. The key is consistency—invest regularly, stay the course, and avoid tinkering when the market gets volatile.

You don't have to do anything fancy. Traditional FI rewards patience, discipline, and time in the market—not perfect timing or high risk. This path is best for people who enjoy their work (enough), value stability, and prefer a simple, data-backed approach to early retirement. It might not be the fastest route, but it's one of the most reliable—and for many, that peace of mind is worth the wait.

## Fat FI

Want to live lavishly? You'll love Fat FI.

Fat FI is traditional financial independence with a generous cushion. It's the version of FI where you can live exactly how you want—travel in style, eat out often, and live comfortably in a high-cost-of-living area, without worrying about money, markets, or budgets.

**The Numbers:** FI Number = Annual Expenses × 25 (e.g. $200,000 × 25 = $5,000,000)

**Pros:**

- Complete freedom and peace of mind during market downturns.
- Provides flexibility for family support, philanthropy, or legacy planning.

**Cons:**

- Takes the longest to reach.

- It can lead to lifestyle creep or burnout from chasing a higher income.

**Next Steps:** Define what "living lavishly" means to you. Is it luxury travel, private school for your kids, early philanthropy, or simply never worrying about money again? Getting clear on what abundance looks like will help you estimate your true Fat FI number.

Once you've defined that lifestyle, reverse engineer it. Figure out how much it costs per year, multiply by 25, and set that as your target. Then work backward: what income, savings rate, or business growth would it take to reach that number in 10, 15, or 20 years?

One important note: many people think they want Fat FI simply because they haven't run the numbers yet. In reality, "lavish" living can cost far less than you might expect. In some places, you can hire a private chef for around $1,000 per month, fly semi-private for a few hundred dollars, or travel the world comfortably for just a few thousand dollars a month. Maybe the life you want truly is expensive—and that's fine. Just make sure you're not sacrificing decades of freedom to chase a number you don't actually need.

Fat FI is best for high earners, entrepreneurs, or families who want financial independence *without* compromise. It's about freedom, comfort, and choice—living abundantly now and in the future, on your own terms.

## Which One Is Right for You?

The best path will depend on your age, your goals, and your risk tolerance, and it doesn't have to stay the same forever. As your life changes, your version of freedom can change with it. What matters most is that you know your numbers and understand what you're working toward.

Whether your target is $5,000 per month in cash flow or $2,000,000 invested, having a clear number helps you measure progress, course-correct when needed, and stay motivated over the long haul. And if you're still unsure about your numbers, flip back to the earlier chapters for a step-by-step breakdown and tools to help you calculate them.

Think of financial independence as a range of options rather than a single destination. You can move between stages, blend different approaches, or redefine what "retirement" means as you go. There's no perfect path—just the one that gives you more control over your time and choices. And there's more than one way to get there.

### CASE STUDY: RACHEL RICHARDS

*Financial freedom age: 27*

Rachel Richards' journey to financial independence is one that illustrates how your path might take unexpected twists and turns. She grew up in a paycheck-to-paycheck household where money was always tight, and those early experiences gave her a deep desire to build a life where she never had to rely on anyone financially. By middle school, she was reading *Rich Dad Poor Dad* and imagining what freedom could look like.

From the beginning, Rachel paired frugality with hustle. She graduated debt-free thanks to scholarships, financial aid, and summers spent selling Cutco knives—often earning around $10,000 each summer. After college, she lived on just $1,500 a month on a $36,000 salary and saved half her income. But the real acceleration came when she dove into real estate. Between 2017 and 2019, she and her then-husband acquired 38 rental units, stacking cash flow on top of the growing royalties from her first book, *Money Honey*. By 2019, she was earning over $10,000 a month from rentals and several thousand more from her books. It was a fast, focused sprint to FI.

Then everything changed. In 2022, Rachel went through a difficult divorce that required selling most of her assets and covering more than $54,000 in legal fees. Essentially, she had to start over. But instead of seeing it as the end of her FI story, she reframed it as a new beginning. She kept investing, leaned into the projects she controlled, and rebuilt her net worth—reaching solo millionaire status again by age 30.

Rachel's path illustrates one of the most important lessons in this chapter: financial independence doesn't follow a straight line. She hit FI once, lost much of what she'd built, and then hit it again through a different combination of income, investing, and lifestyle choices. Her story shows that there are countless routes to FI, and the real key is staying committed to the goal, adjusting when life shifts, and continuing to execute your plan—even when the plan needs to evolve.

Today, Rachel splits her time between Denver summers and warm-weather travel in the winter. She fills her days with creative writing courses, volunteering, fostering puppies, salsa dancing in Colombia, taking Italian classes in Sicily, and running fitness challenges with friends. She describes her life now as joyful, healthy, and deeply aligned with her values. Her journey is a reminder that FI isn't a single destination—it's a direction, and sometimes a path you navigate more than once.

## Call to Action: Determine Your FI Strategy

Take a few minutes right now to identify which version of FI feels most appealing to you. Do constant mini-retirements sound like your dream? Maybe coasting to FI and stopping contributions early? Or picking up a part-time job for health insurance with Barista FI? Perhaps building passive income through Cash Flow FI—or going the nest-egg-only route with Lean, Traditional, or Fat FI?

You don't have to lock yourself into just one path, but choose the version that excites you the most. Once you've identified it, set a concrete goal—whether that's increasing your savings rate, launching a new income stream, or simply running your numbers—and start making moves toward it.

# CHAPTER 17

# WITHDRAWAL STRATEGIES

*"Every new beginning comes from some other beginning's end."*

— SENECA

You've reached your FI number, your accounts are full, and your portfolio is built. But now comes the most important question: how do you actually live off your investments? Even if you take a hybrid approach—covering part of your lifestyle with cash flow from real estate, a small business, or other income sources—there will likely come a time when you need to start withdrawing from your investment portfolio to help cover your expenses.

This chapter breaks down how to turn that nest egg into a sustainable income stream. Whether you're retiring at 30 or

65, you need a strategy that allows you to spend your money wisely without running out.

We'll explore drawdown strategies, account sequencing, how taxes play into the equation, and how your withdrawal plan may vary depending on the type of early retirement you choose.

## Withdrawal Order: A Strategic Framework

When it's time to start pulling money from your accounts, order matters. Here's a commonly used framework among early retirees:

*1. Taxable Brokerage Accounts*

These are usually the first to tap because they're the most flexible. You've already paid taxes on the money you contributed, so you'll only owe taxes on the *gains*—and if those are long-term (held over a year), they're taxed at much lower rates than ordinary income. For many early retirees, this often means paying little to no federal tax at all, especially if your total income stays below the long-term capital gains threshold. Selling from your taxable accounts also gives your retirement accounts more time to grow untouched.

*2. Roth IRA Contributions*

Next, you can dip into your Roth IRA contributions (not earnings) at any time, tax- and penalty-free. Think of this as your built-in safety valve. It's a great backup source of funds for unexpected expenses or to bridge small income gaps without triggering additional taxes.

### 3. Roth Conversions (laddered)

If you've been using a Roth conversion ladder (explained in the next section), you'll want to start drawing from the oldest conversions once their individual five-year clocks have expired. The goal is to "ladder" these conversions so every year, a new chunk becomes available tax-free. This approach smooths out taxes over time and gives you access to funds well before age 59½ without penalties.

### 4. Traditional Retirement Accounts (401(k)s, IRAs)

These accounts are designed for long-term use. Once you hit 59½, you can start withdrawing without penalties (though you'll still owe income tax on the withdrawals). Until then, these funds are best left alone to keep compounding. Later in retirement, you can strategically draw from these accounts to fill in any remaining income needs or balance your tax brackets.

### 5. Social Security, Pensions, and Annuities

If you qualify for any of these, delaying them can often pay off. For example, every year you delay Social Security (up to age 70) increases your monthly benefit by about 8% per year (not inflation-adjusted). Think of this as a guaranteed return that's hard to beat anywhere else. They typically aren't part of the early retirement phase, but can become an important backstop later, if available.

### Putting It All Together

This order works because it prioritizes flexibility and minimizes taxes. You start by withdrawing from the accounts that trigger the least tax burden, while giving your tax-advantaged accounts the longest possible runway to grow.

Now, you might be wondering, "How do I actually access some of these retirement funds without getting hit with early withdrawal penalties?" Great question—let's dive into that next.

## Accessing Retirement Funds Early

If you're retiring early, chances are a big chunk of your wealth is tied up in tax-advantaged accounts—401(k)s, IRAs—that aren't designed to be touched until age 59½. A lot of people avoid these accounts altogether because they assume the money is "locked up until retirement."

But that's not entirely true. There are plenty of ways to legally access your funds early without paying that dreaded 10% penalty. You just have to plan ahead. Here are some of the most common (and effective) strategies:

### *Roth Conversion Ladders*

This strategy involves moving money from a Traditional IRA or 401(k) into a Roth IRA over a series of years. Each conversion starts its own five-year clock, and once that clock expires, the converted funds can be withdrawn tax- and penalty-free, even if you're under age 59½. To use this strategy smoothly, you need to begin conversions at least five years before you plan to live on them, creating a "ladder" where a new chunk becomes available each year.

### 72(t) SEPP (Substantially Equal Periodic Payments)

This strategy allows you to take early withdrawals from an IRA (or sometimes a 401(k)) without penalty, as long as you commit to a fixed withdrawal schedule for at least five years or until you reach age 59½—whichever comes later. It's a bit rigid and technical, but it can be a powerful tool for predictable income during early retirement.

### Rule of 55

If you leave your job in or after the year you turn 55 (or 50 for certain public safety employees), you can withdraw from your current employer's 401(k) without paying the 10% penalty. The catch? The money has to stay in that specific employer's plan—you can't roll it into an IRA first.

### 457(b) Plans

If you work for the government or a nonprofit, you might have access to a 457(b) plan. These are unique because you can withdraw funds penalty-free as soon as you leave your job, regardless of age. That makes them one of the most flexible retirement accounts out there for early retirees.

### Inherited IRAs

If you inherit an IRA, the rules are different. Most non-spouse beneficiaries must withdraw the entire balance within 10 years—but there are no early withdrawal penalties, no matter your age. While this isn't something you can plan around, it's useful to understand if you ever find yourself managing an inherited account.

*Portfolio Loans (Taxable Accounts Only)*

Even though this isn't technically a way to access your retirement money early, it's a strategy that lets you keep your investments compounding in the market while freeing up cash to use elsewhere.

If you have a large taxable brokerage account, some brokerages allow you to borrow against your investments through what's called a margin loan or securities-backed line of credit (SBLOC). For example, if you have $1 million invested, you might be able to borrow $200,000 against it without selling any shares, meaning you won't trigger capital gains taxes. It's not risk-free—if your investments drop enough in value, the brokerage can require you to add more cash or sell investments to pay down the loan—but it can be a useful bridge strategy for early retirees who want liquidity without selling assets.

*Or, Don't Withdraw Early At All*

If you really want to let your money compound for decades, pick a strategy that gives you that flexibility. Maybe you take extended mini-retirements every few years, but keep working in between. Or you lean into Coast FI and work just enough to cover your expenses. Or maybe you focus on Cash Flow FI and let your investments grow untouched. There's no single "right" path here—it's a choose-your-own-adventure. My goal is simply to give you the tools and knowledge to make those choices with confidence.

If you do decide to start withdrawing from your portfolio, though, it's important to understand one of the biggest threats to any early retirement plan.

## Sequence of Returns Risk

One of the most important concepts to understand when creating a withdrawal strategy is the *sequence of returns risk*.

Here's the basic idea: two people could retire with the exact same portfolio—say $1 million—and both earn the same average annual return over 30 years. But if one of them experiences strong market gains in the first few years while the other gets hit with a market crash early on, their outcomes will look drastically different.

Why? Because early losses hurt more. When the market drops at the beginning of retirement, your portfolio shrinks before it has a chance to grow again. And if you're withdrawing money during that downturn, you're selling at low prices—locking in losses and leaving less invested to recover later.

Let's look at two retirees, Alex and Jordan. Both retire with $1 million, plan to withdraw $40,000 per year (a 4% withdrawal rate), and both average a 7% annual return over 30 years. The only difference? *When* the bad years happen.

- Right after Jordan retires, the market enters a long bull run.

- Right after Alex retires, the market collapses into a major bear market.

Even though their portfolios earn the same average return over time, the sequence of those returns changes everything.

In Alex's first three years of retirement, the market drops nearly 40%. Between withdrawals and market losses, his portfolio falls to roughly $600,000 by year three. Even when the market rebounds, he's now withdrawing from a much smaller base, and his money has to work harder just to recover. By year 25, Alex's portfolio is nearly depleted.

Jordan, on the other hand, retires into strong early market growth. His $1 million portfolio grows to $1.3 million even while withdrawing $40,000 per year. By the time the next bear market rolls around, his portfolio has a substantial cushion, so he doesn't need to tighten spending or make major adjustments to his plan. Same returns. Same withdrawals. Drastically different outcomes—all because of timing.

That's the sequence of returns risk in action. You can't control when the market dips, but you can control how much you withdraw, how diversified you are, and how big your safety buffer is.

If you want to see how different market scenarios could impact your plan, search "retirement simulation calculators" and start punching in numbers. There are plenty of tools and websites, such as ProjectionLab, that let you stress test your portfolio against historical market data and visualize how your money might hold up through both booms and crashes.

*Breaking the 4% Rule*

The 4% rule gets thrown around a lot in the financial independence community. It's the idea that you can safely withdraw 4% of your portfolio in the first year of retirement, then adjust that amount each year for inflation—without ever running out of money. But that doesn't mean you *have* to pull exactly 4% every single year, no matter what the market's doing. Real life isn't that rigid, and neither should your plan be.

My friend Brandon Ganch, better known as *The Mad Fientist*, retired at 34 and recommends an approach called a flexible discretionary spending model. Essential expenses—housing, food, insurance—are always covered. But "fun money" flexes with the market.

In a great year, when your portfolio grows, you could spend an extra $20,000 on travel or experiences. In a down year, you might dial back to $5,000 or $10,000. It's a simple but powerful way to protect your portfolio without feeling like you're sacrificing everything.

He also recommends building your FI number around your *core expenses*—the non-negotiables that keep the lights on and food on the table—and treating everything else as optional. This way, your basic needs are always covered, and you can adjust lifestyle spending as markets fluctuate.

Having that bit of flexibility makes your plan far more sustainable—both financially and emotionally. You're less likely to panic during a market downturn, and your odds of long-term success go way up.

And remember, if you retire early, you still have options. During rough years, you can always pick up a small side hustle, take on a short-term consulting project, or earn a little income doing something fun. That's the beauty of early retirement—you've bought yourself time and freedom. If you need to earn again for a season, it's by choice, not necessity. As Joel from FI 180 would say "Your worst-case scenario is everybody else's everyday scenario."

### Building a Cash Buffer

Another simple way to protect yourself from sequence of returns risk is to build a cash buffer—essentially, a stash of cash or low-volatility investments that can cover your expenses for a few years. Think of it as a shock absorber for your portfolio. During market downturns, instead of selling stocks at a loss, you can pull from this cash reserve to fund your lifestyle. Then, when the market recovers, you can replenish the buffer by selling appreciated assets at better prices.

How much to keep depends on your comfort level and income stability. Many early retirees hold between one and three years' worth of expenses in cash, short-term bonds, or high-yield savings. For example, if your annual expenses are $60,000, you might set aside $120,000 in a high-yield savings account or in government bonds. That gives your stock investments time to rebound without forcing you to sell at the worst possible time.

This strategy is especially powerful during the first few years of retirement—the "danger zone"—where early losses have the biggest long-term impact. A healthy cash buffer can smooth out the ride, reduce stress, and help you stay invested through market turbulence.

If you're transitioning into early retirement, start building your cash buffer in the final year or two of work. Gradually shift a small portion of your portfolio from stocks into cash or bonds so that you're ready when your paychecks stop coming in.

Remember, this isn't about timing the market—it's about buying yourself time *in* the market, and avoiding forced withdrawals. A good buffer keeps you calm, consistent, and confident, no matter what the headlines say.

## How Real People Draw Down

Once you've built your portfolio and hit your FI number, the next big question becomes: how do you *actually* spend it down? Most people focus so much on *getting to* financial independence that they forget there's a strategy to living from it.

The key is sequencing. Which accounts you tap—and when—can drastically affect your taxes, your portfolio's longevity, and your peace of mind. Let's look at three examples of how this might play out in real life.

### Bridget – The Bridge Strategy

Bridget hit FI at 32 with a $1 million portfolio spread across a taxable brokerage account, Roth IRA, and 401(k). Since she's decades away from traditional retirement age, she needs a plan to bridge the gap between now and when she can access her retirement accounts penalty-free.

Here's how she does it:

- **Years 1–2:** Bridget lives off a mix of cash and her taxable brokerage account. She keeps about two years of living expenses (roughly $80,000) in a high-yield savings account and short-term bonds, giving her flexibility no matter what the market does.

- **Years 3–10:** She continues drawing from her taxable account, selling appreciated shares strategically to stay in the 0% long-term capital gains bracket.

- **Meanwhile:** Each year, she's converting a chunk of her traditional 401(k) into her Roth IRA—a Roth conversion ladder. By year six, the first Roth conversions have cleared the five-year rule and are available tax- and penalty-free.

- **Beyond year 10:** Bridget now has full access to her Roth funds and continues drawing from a mix of Roth and brokerage accounts while letting her remaining investments compound.

Bridget's approach gives her incredible flexibility. She never touches her 401(k) directly, minimizes taxes, and ensures her money keeps growing while she enjoys her 30s and 40s.

Her focus: longevity, tax-efficiency, and letting compounding do the heavy lifting.

*Bob – The Barbell Strategy*

Bob left his engineering job at 43 with $1.5 million invested and a small consulting business that brings in $30,000 a year.

His income covers about half of his expenses, so his portfolio doesn't have to work as hard.

His drawdown approach looks like this:

- **Ongoing:** Bob covers day-to-day expenses with consulting income plus small withdrawals from his taxable brokerage account.

- **Each year:** He uses Roth conversions to intentionally fill the lower tax brackets (10% and 12%), moving just enough from his Traditional IRA to his Roth without spilling into the next bracket.

- **Cash buffer:** He keeps two years of expenses in a money market fund, allowing him to pause withdrawals during bad market years.

- **Down the road:** When consulting slows down, he can live off his taxable and Roth accounts until he reaches 59½, then tap his traditional accounts penalty-free.

Bob's plan is what I'd call a "barbell" strategy. He's balancing a small stream of earned income on one side with tax-optimized portfolio withdrawals on the other. He enjoys flexibility, avoids sequence of returns risk, and still gets the satisfaction of occasional work.

His focus: stability, control, and long-term tax optimization.

*Glenda – The Glidepath Strategy*

Glenda retired at 55 after 30 years in corporate management with $2 million—most of it in tax-deferred retirement accounts. Her main challenge isn't running out of money; it's figuring out how to access it efficiently before RMDs (Required Minimum Distributions) kick in at 73.

Here's how her drawdown plan looks:

- **Years 1–5:** Glenda uses a mix of cash savings and the Rule of 55 to withdraw from her current employer's 401(k) without penalty (since she left her job at or after age 55).

- **Years 6–15:** Once she rolls that 401(k) into an IRA, she begins annual Roth conversions, gradually shifting money from her traditional accounts to her Roth to lower future RMDs.

- **Throughout:** She keeps a three-year cash buffer— roughly $240,000—to cover expenses during market downturns and avoid selling stocks at a loss.

- **At 70+:** Social Security kicks in, reducing her withdrawal needs even further, and her Roth IRA continues compounding tax-free for later years (or as a legacy for her kids).

Glenda's plan is simple and steady. She's not chasing every optimization, but she's making smart moves that minimize taxes, keep income consistent, and protect against market shocks.

Her focus: simplicity, access, and risk management.

Each of these examples uses the same basic tools—cash buffers, Roth conversions, taxable accounts—but in different combinations depending on their timelines, income needs, and goals. There's no single "right" way to draw down your portfolio. But there *is* a right way for *you*—the one that balances taxes, flexibility, and peace of mind while letting your money continue to grow in the background.

## Call to Action: Plan Your Withdrawal Strategy

Every journey to FI needs a solid exit plan. Don't just focus on building wealth—create a strategy to *use* it wisely. A thoughtful drawdown plan is just as important as your accumulation strategy, and ensures your money lasts as long as you need it to.

And remember, your plan doesn't have to be perfect—it just has to exist. It's far better to have a flexible plan that evolves than no plan at all. Too many people race toward FI without a roadmap for how they'll actually live off their portfolio once they get there.

# CHAPTER 18

# LIFE IN RETIREMENT

*"Don't simply retire from something; have something
to retire to."*

— HENRY EMERSON FOSDICK

Financial independence solves the money problem, but
it doesn't automatically solve the life problem. Once your
expenses are covered—by investments, cash flow, or both—
you're free from the obligation to work. But now what? Do you
spend your days watching Netflix? Sipping margaritas on the
beach? If that truly fulfills you, go for it. But most people who
make it this far don't just sit around and do nothing.

Early retirement isn't the finish line. It's the starting point for
something bigger. It's your chance to reinvent yourself. Knock
things off your to-do list that have been sitting there for years
(or decades). Go on adventures. Build that business. Spend

more time with loved ones. Learn that instrument. Get in the best shape of your life. The world is your oyster.

What most people don't tell you is that freedom can be *scary*. Once money isn't an issue and you have complete control over your time, there's no one left to blame. No more "lack of free time." No more "crazy work schedule." Anything you don't do—after saying you'd do it—is on you. Still haven't run that marathon? That's on you. Still haven't learned Spanish? On you. Still haven't booked that European trip you've been dreaming about for decades? Yep. On you.

I struggled with this for a while after reaching financial independence. It felt overwhelming. So… I can just do *anything*? It sounds amazing, but without a plan, that level of freedom can also create stress and anxiety. That's why it's important to practice what your life in retirement will actually look like—before you get there.

## Practicing Retirement

We like to think of money as this abstract thing, but in reality, money is just a tool. As you accumulate more of it, you gain the ability to use it to build the life you've always wanted. That's why I'm a huge proponent of building the habits, relationships, goals, skills, and routines you want *now*—and slowly adding more of them as you progress along your FI journey. Practicing retirement means building your future life before you quit working, so the transition feels natural instead of overwhelming.

If your goal is to get really good at guitar in retirement, start playing for ten to fifteen minutes a day now (or as much as you can). If you want to get in the best shape of your life, start going to the gym and eating better today. If becoming fluent in French is on your list, start learning a little here and there. When retirement finally arrives, the habits are already there—you're just turning up the dial with all your newfound free time.

Early retirement is incredible, but you need something to retire *to*. If your life is completely consumed by work right up until the day you reach financial independence—and then you quit cold turkey—those first few months of freedom can feel disorienting. I know early retirees who went back to work simply because they were bored. They didn't practice retirement—they removed work without replacing it with anything meaningful.

If you skipped it, go back to the exercise in Chapter 2 where I asked you to write down the ten things you value most— and actually do it this time. If you already did it, review your answers. This is how you practice retirement. Only you know what an ideal day, week, month, and year look like, so start adjusting your schedule now.

Do this well, and over time you'll build a life—and a schedule— that's as aligned as possible with what you value most.

## Your Ideal Day

Another exercise that was incredibly helpful for Lauren and me after reaching financial independence was envisioning our ideal day. Not every day has to look exactly the same, of course, but having a clear sense of what an ideal day includes makes it much easier to structure your time intentionally.

You probably won't know what your ideal day looks like right away—and that's normal. This takes experimentation. Try different routines, activities, and schedules. You'll know when something feels "right." Keep iterating and tweaking until you find a rhythm that excites you. This process took us a while, but today we have a pretty solid sense of what a great day looks like for us. Our weekends tend to be a bit more hectic, but here's what a typical weekday looks like:

- **7:00 AM–9:30 AM:** Gym and/or something active like running or walking

- **9:30 AM–10:00 AM:** Morning smoothie and practicing Spanish

- **10:00 AM–12:30 PM:** Work on our businesses or other projects

- **12:30 PM–1:00 PM:** Lunch

- **1:00 PM–2:00 PM:** Afternoon walk

- **2:00 PM–6:00 PM:** More work, projects, or business-related tasks

- **6:00 PM–6:15 PM:** Mini-workout before dinner

- **6:15 PM–7:00 PM:** Cook and eat dinner together

- **7:00 PM–9:30 PM:** Hang out with friends, plan trips, watch TV, talk, etc.
- **9:30 PM–10:00 PM:** Read for a bit, then head to bed

Does this happen every single day? Of course not. But we try to come pretty close. Our goal is to stack as many "good" days as possible. If something stops feeling good, we cut it. If something feels missing, we add it. Your ideal day doesn't have to be rigid or set in stone.

I know this will change once we have kids—and that's okay. I fully expect our ideal day to evolve over the years and decades. What matters most is having open communication about what makes us feel happy and fulfilled. This is something we revisit often during our monthly check-ins, and we make adjustments as needed.

One thing you might have noticed is that work still shows up in my ideal day, which may have surprised you. Believe it or not, I actually enjoy working. I like having a goal to work toward, creating things, and feeling like I'm having an impact. If I ever lose those feelings, I'll stop. That's the key difference: I'm working because I *want* to, not because I *have* to.

## When Work Becomes Optional

Even though this book is called *Retire by 30*, it's more like *Reach Financial Independence Really Fast Then Do Whatever You Want*—but that title wasn't quite as catchy. You don't actually have to retire, and you don't have to do it by age 30. The real goal of this book is to help you reach financial independence as quickly as possible. Once you do, work becomes optional—and that changes everything.

When you don't *need* a paycheck, the pressure disappears. You can work less. You can work on things you actually care about. You can walk away the moment something stops feeling aligned. Or you can stop working entirely. There's no right answer. Only the one that feels right for you.

For a lot of people, myself included, financial independence doesn't mean never working again. It means choosing *how, when,* and *why* you work. It's the difference between building your life around a job and fitting work into a life you've intentionally designed.

As Morgan Housel puts it in *The Psychology of Money*, "The ability to do what you want, when you want, with who you want, for as long as you want, is priceless."

For many people, the hardest part isn't reaching financial independence. It's figuring out who they are once they get there. When work has dictated your schedule, your identity, and your sense of progress for decades, removing that structure can feel disorienting at first. That's normal. There's often a decompression period where you need to slow down before you can see clearly what you actually want.

The good news is that you don't have to decide what the rest of your life looks like the moment you hit your FI number. Life after financial independence tends to happen in seasons. You might work a lot for a while, then not at all. You might take a year off, then start something new.

Personally, I like to work in seasons. Some months, I'll work 40+ hours a week for several weeks straight. Other months, I might travel around Europe and work just five hours per week. If I feel like working more, I do. If I don't, I don't.

Optional work can take many forms. Some people consult for a few hours a week. Others teach, mentor, or build passion projects without worrying whether they'll make money. Some take long breaks between projects. And some decide they're done working altogether. None of these paths is better than the others. Financial independence simply gives you the flexibility to choose what fits your life right now, and to change your mind later.

## Money Only Solves Money Problems

You've probably heard the phrase "money doesn't buy happiness," and it's true. But money *does* solve money problems—and that matters more than people like to admit. If your living situation feels unstable, you're stressed about your car breaking down, or you're unsure how you'll afford groceries next month, money can absolutely reduce anxiety and buy you peace of mind. In those situations, more money can be life-changing. It creates breathing room. It lowers stress. It gives you the mental space to think about something other than survival.

What money *doesn't* do is automatically make you fulfilled. Once your basic financial needs are met, happiness stops being a money problem and starts becoming a life problem. That's where things like practicing retirement and envisioning your ideal day come into play. If you don't know what you're working *toward*, no amount of money will suddenly give you purpose when you arrive.

I've seen this play out firsthand. I know people with more than $10,000,000 in net worth who complain constantly and carry a generally negative outlook on life. I also know people with less than $100,000 who are genuinely happy, optimistic, and fulfilled. Jim Carrey summed it up perfectly when he said, "I think everybody should get rich and famous and do everything they ever dreamed of so they can see that it's not the answer." Money can remove obstacles, but it can't tell you what actually matters to you.

That's why it's so important to have something to retire *to*, not just something to retire *from*. If you postpone fulfillment until after you reach financial independence, you're setting yourself up for disappointment. The habits, relationships, interests, and sense of purpose you want later should start showing up in your life now—long before you hit your FI number.

The money part is important. That's why I wrote this book. Financial independence gives you options, flexibility, and freedom, but it's not the destination. It's the starting point. It's the beginning of a life where money no longer dictates every decision you make—a life where you can choose how to spend your time based on what you enjoy, not what pays the bills. So while money doesn't buy happiness, having enough of it gives you the space to focus on the things that actually do.

## Action = Results

If you made it this far, you've spent hours learning how to reduce expenses, increase income, invest wisely, optimize taxes, and design a life you actually want to live. But learning and doing are two very different things. You might have read five books before this and changed nothing, or maybe you already have five more lined up. One thing I've learned along the way is that there *is* such a thing as too much information.

You can read all the books, listen to all the podcasts, and watch all the videos—but the thing that creates real results is action. You don't need to do everything in this book. I've given you a massive menu of options. Acting on just a few of them could dramatically change your financial future. Building wealth doesn't have to be complicated. In fact, if I had to boil this entire book down to five words, they would be this:

*Spend less. Earn more. Invest.*

Optimizing your expenses will grow your gap. Maximizing your income will accelerate your path. Learning how to invest properly will compound your progress. But taking *any* action from what you've learned will put you ahead of the vast majority of people. I included calls to action at the end of most chapters (and I truly hope you do them), but even if you only complete half, your future self will thank you.

I hope that this book helps you reach financial independence sooner than you ever thought possible—and that you use that freedom to build a life you genuinely love. Even today, five years after reaching FI, I still have moments where I stop and think, *How is this real?* Some days, it hasn't fully sunk in, but none of it happened by accident. It only happened because, at some point, I decided to take action.

I want the same for you. No matter your background, age, race, gender, education, or connections, financial independence is possible for you.

Action creates momentum. And momentum changes lives. So when you finish this book, don't just forget about it and move on to the next thing. Take action. Do something—anything—different. You might just start a domino effect that leads you all the way to financial freedom.

# RETIRE BY 30 RESOURCES (FREE)

To access all the resources mentioned in this book—websites, calculators, tools, and more—scan the QR code below to grab your FREE copy.

# ABOUT THE AUTHOR

Cody Berman is an entrepreneur, real estate investor, and personal finance educator. After reaching financial independence at age 25 through online business, strategic investing, and intentional living, he made it his mission to help others achieve freedom on their own terms. He's the creator of an award-winning personal finance podcast and has built multiple seven-figure businesses that generate passive income. When he's not teaching others how to build wealth, you'll find him traveling the world, in the gym, or launching his next business venture.

# HELP ME OUT?

**Thank you for reading my book!**

If this book helped you in any way, I'd really appreciate it if you took two minutes to leave a review on Amazon. Your support helps spread the word and helps others decide if this is the right book for them.

**Thanks so much!**

**- Cody**